当组织中人手一本

《高效会议指南：1 小时就能读懂的会议议事规则（第 10 版）》

会议可以开得更好！

高效会议指南：
1 小时就能读懂的会议议事规则（第 10 版）

【加】弗雷德·弗朗西斯
【加】佩格·弗朗西斯 著

刘员外 译

浙江人民出版社

图书在版编目（CIP）数据

浙江省版权局
著作权合同登记章
图字：11-2019-281号

高效会议指南 ：1小时就能读懂的会议议事规则 ：第10版 / （加）弗雷德·弗朗西斯，（加）佩格·弗朗西斯著 ；刘员外译. -- 杭州 ：浙江人民出版社，2020. 7
书名原文：Democratic Rules of Order
ISBN 978-7-213-09751-5

Ⅰ. ①高… Ⅱ. ①弗… ②佩… ③刘… Ⅲ. ①会议－组织管理学 Ⅳ. ①C931. 47

中国版本图书馆 CIP 数据核字 (2020) 第 095496 号

高效会议指南：1 小时就能读懂的会议议事规则（第 10 版）

[加] 弗雷德·弗朗西斯 [加] 佩格·弗朗西斯 著 刘员外 译

出版发行：浙江人民出版社（杭州市体育场路 347 号邮编 310006）
市场部电话：（0571）85061682 85176516
责任编辑：丁谨之 何英娇
营销编辑：陈雯怡 陈芊如
责任校对：陈 春
责任印务：聂绪东
封面设计：南京观止堂文化发展有限公司
电脑制版：南京观止堂文化发展有限公司
印 刷：北京阳光印易科技有限公司
开 本：787 毫米 ×1092 毫米 1/32 印 张：5
字 数：77 千字 插 页：4
版 次：2020 年 7 月第 1 版 印 次：2020 年 7 月第 1 次印刷
书 号：ISBN 978-7-213-09751-5
定 价：48.00 元

如发现印装质量问题，影响阅读，请与市场部联系调换。

好评推荐

你们的会议是否开得低效、令人沮丧，甚至不合议事规则？《高效会议指南：1 小时就能读懂的会议议事规则（第 10 版）》是一本充满智慧的小书，可以向你开启一个不同的世界。每个人都应该买一本，这将是最有价值的投资之一。

——布鲁斯·巴彻列（Bruce Batchelor），作家、出版商、创新者、不再对开会感到沮丧的参会者

这是《罗伯特议事规则》（*Robert's Rules of Order*）的简化版、现代版，比《罗伯特议事规则》更清晰，更适合当今社会，助力举行人性化高效会议。

——里格·哥特，PCC 媒体制作 /PCC-TV，西尔韦尼亚波特兰社区大学教育咨询委员会主席团成员

很多社区的管理者都陷入了《罗伯特议事规则》的复杂之中，因此我们团队和温哥华岛地产所有者协会（VISOA）向各阶层推荐这本不复杂的《高效会议指南：1 小时就能读懂的会议议事规则（第 10 版）》。

——大卫·格鲁伯（David Grubb），温哥华岛地产所有者协会地产支持团队董事会成员与主席

我们向所有机构和组织强烈推荐这本书，因为它给出了一个明确、简单的会议指导。

——卡罗琳·何慕（Caroline Holm），加拿大维多利亚基督教科学派文书、第一教堂牧师

这本易用的指南可以让我们处理好要做的工作，避免经常因跑题而陷入混乱。向作者致敬，这本书让深陷杂乱无序会议中的我们重回正轨。

——彼得·沃斯特（Pieter Vorster），库特奈橄榄球队董事会成员，TideChange.ca 总编辑

我给每位董事会成员买了一本《高效会议指南：1 小时就能读懂的会议议事规则（第 10 版）》。我们通过投票让这本书成为我们公司的官方会议流程手册。这本书具有以下特点：

（1）易懂；（2）易学；（3）易用；（4）逻辑性强；（5）高效。

——爱德华·E．道格拉斯（Edward E. Douglas），信托信息董事会原副主席

对我们所有人来说，这是一本真正的指南……它为三个挑战提供了优雅的解决方案：如何公平、高效和秩序良好地召开会议，如何以人人都能理解的规则行事，以及如何在一个比以往任何时候都更需要民主的世界中培育真正的民主气氛。

——吉姆·雷姆德（Jim Rietmulder），作家，《当孩子管理学校时》（*When Kids Rule the School*）作者，圈子学校共同创始人

这本书是高效开会最好的参考书，书中的会议术语很实用。全书结构严谨，内容细致，信息量大。

——格里·奥沙利文（Gerry O' Sullivan），引导者、调解员、培训师、《协调员的工具箱》（*The Mediator's Toolkit*）作者

目　录

序　言

弗雷德·弗朗西斯和佩格·弗朗西斯做了一件很棒的事。他们的这本书，对任何规格和级别的会议——上至国家级会议，下至社区会议的主持人和参加民主讨论的人，都是不可或缺的。弗朗西斯夫妇的成功之处就在于，他们将会议程序删繁就简，将其简化为一套任何人都能遵循的常识规则。使用这本书后，你对会议效果的失望感会大大降低，同时会使会议的民主参与程度大大提高。

这些年来，我主持或参加了政府、企业、教会和社会各级组织召开的数百次会议，经常因主持会议的困难而感到沮丧。这些困难包括要使每个参会者都能理解会议议程，让多数人的意志能够形成决议并占上风。许多困难源于这样一个事实，即很少有人有时间或意愿去研究陈腐的会议规则方面的书籍，因此很容易被懂得会议规则的极少数人诱导，有时甚至被他们摆布。

弗朗西斯夫妇的这本书对民主议事做出了重要贡献。它可以随时被各种团体、委员会、工会或者集团公司采用，并将为其带来持久的利益。就我个人而言，多年来，我一直参加议会辩论，已深刻认识到在民主议事程序中通过制定规则和遵循规则来达成共识的价值和必要性。然而，到目前为止，这些规则极其复杂，常常令人困惑，而且在许多层面上都令人不满意。从现在起，那些采用《高效会议指南：1 小时就能读懂的会议议事规则（第 10 版）》的团体将会发现，他们的会议主旨的贯彻程度和会议结果的有效性都将得到显著的提高和改善。

道格拉斯·莱特曼（Douglas Leiterman）
索瑟姆新闻的议会记者
加拿大广播公司（CBC）执行制作人
电影债券公司首席执行官

前　言

你是否因会议缺乏效率而感到沮丧。例如很难顺利推动会议议程，或由于情绪失控而使会议秩序混乱、使自己丧失专业性，又或者未能促使能真正代表与会者愿望的建设性决策通过……

不止你一个人有这样的感觉。然而事情本不应该这样！

在从事多年的社团志愿服务——包括参加了数以百计场次的专业和非营利会议后，弗雷德·弗朗西斯和佩格·弗朗西斯意识到，有一个简明、权威的高效会议指南是多么必要——能帮助公司董事会、各种委员会和其他团体成员，通过举办高效、实现预期效果的会议来公平地达成与会者的共识。

他们无法找到类似的会议指南，所以决定自己撰写一本这样的会议议事规则。经过几年的努力，他们不断修改和完善（其中包括参考了行政人员、政府议员和其他用户提出的大量建议），确保其中的每一点都非常清楚，没有遗漏任何一条必要的规则，最后终于将这份会议议事规则制定出来了。1994 年，《高效会议易用指南》（*Distinctly Democratic Rules of Order*）正式出版，后来改名为《会议易用指南》（*Democratic Rules of Order*）。这本简单易用的手册已经成为受人尊敬和有价值的参考书，供成千上万个大大小小的组织使用，也供世界各地的学生在课堂上学习民主议事流程。

不同团体的使用情况

本书运用从工会、专业协会到各级委员会、教会和非政府组织，甚至包括虚拟平台会议等各类会议，是一本会议议事规则的“袖珍指南”。它规定会议应按一个循序渐进的过程进行，允许所有成员参与交换意见和集体决策。

这本书有意被设计为袖珍型，可以在不到

1 小时的时间内读完，甚至在会议出现相关问题时，人们可以将其携带到会议现场作为参考。

易用格式

为了便于阅读，我们将本书分为两部分。

第一部分：规则——描述组织结构和成员的角色，包括处理任何会议最关键部分的步骤，即决策过程。它有助于读者在会议进程中遵循以下步骤：

· 介绍想法；
· 提出议案和修正案；
· 处理异议和干扰点；
· 管理表决程序；
· 与委员会合作。

第二部分：进一步的帮助——提供其他重要参考信息，包括：

· 常见问题；
· 运用了本书所有关键要素的一次会议脚本示例；
· 说明议事规则的流程图；

· 议事规则的摘要，以便在会议期间快速查阅。

自 1996 年以来，这本书在加拿大持续畅销。这是第 10 版。通过多次修订，作者希望吸引更多的读者购买并阅读这本书，从而帮助人们不断改进会议议事规则，做出更好的决策，进而让世界变得更加美好。

第一部分 规则

规则介绍

公正和秩序

这些议事规则有助于人们共同讨论和考虑各种各样的意见，然后尽可能明智、公平和顺利地做出决定。这些规则适用于没有任何政党之争的任何规模的会议。会议的理想状态是决策基于对事实的客观分析，而不受情绪、群体压力或不必要的协议的影响。作者写作这本书的目的就是帮助人们实现这种理想。

民主原则

这本书不是其他书的简略本。它是一套源于普遍实践和民主自然法则的完整规则，正如《韦伯斯特字典》所说的，“由规则所规定”。这些不言而喻的原则，适用于会议决策，具体包括：

· 每个成员都有权平等和充分地参加不受恐吓、阻挠和其他干扰的有秩序的会议；无论是否出席会议，所有成员都遵守同样容易理解的规则，包括平等和充分地了解所有事件的权利。

· 成员中的多数人有权进行决策（少数服从多数的意思——译者注）。

一种民主理想

我们应记住，我们都属于同一个组织，有着共同的目标。我们可以有各种不同观点，但仍然应该为共同的利益而共同努力，而不是分裂成对立的几方，每个人都各行其是。我们要仔细倾听其他人提出的建议，然后做出自己的决定，这样我们才能最大可能地做出有利的决定。

另一种民主理想

如果面对的是一个错误的决定，我们要接受它吗？要么接受，要么不接受。接受，是为了实践民主表决的结果，我们必须接受合法的决定，并且按照它的要求去做；不接受，是因为我们不需要改变自己的观点。在未来的某一天，我们可能有机会重新审视这个决定，那时或许会发现这个决定竟是好的！

正式程度

在小型团队或关系密切的团队中，通常可以通过达成一致意见进行决策，只要主持人或秘书长记录每个决定，保证所有成员同意即可。

更大的团队也常常非正式地做出决定。推动者让与会成员能以快速、简单的方式做出决定。如果意见产生分歧，则需要一个更加正式的修正秩序。正式程度一般取决于习惯、协议或下一阶段的规则。

更高层级的法律

土地法、宪法、地方法规或者现有的章程可以自动支配议事规则。在这本书中，我们把这些都称为“法律”。

议事规则只适用于会议行为。它们不解释法律，也不弥补地方法规、章程的缺陷。

少数人权益

当民主的多数规则体系与少数人权益产生冲突时，请记住，有更高一层的法律可以保护少数人的权益。几乎所有国家都有法律保护个人的自然权益，包括联合国的《世界人权宣言》。任何团体的决定都不可以侵害广泛受到保护的人权和基本自由权。

达到最高效率

在会议中分享决定流程就像开车一样，需要学习必要的规则和技能。一旦做出了群体决定，决定就成为第二性的。如果每位成员都至少透彻地读一遍这本书，主持人至少读两遍，并且都同意遵守这些规则，那么你们的会议将会像有经验的司机开车一样，可以自如地驾驶，而不需要刻意去想该踩哪个踏板。

关于第 10 版

第 10 版和以前的每一版一样，通过精心地修订，使内容更加清晰、实用、高效。然而，所有版本中的守则都是相似的，所以各个组织可以将之前的版本同最新的版本一起使用，它们之间没有冲突。

虚拟会议

如有必要，对这些规则加以修改后，就可以将其用于电话或视频会议，包括互联网会议。这些会议是通过电子方式进行讨论和投票的。

采纳或修改这些议事规则

一些组织可以在常规规则或附则中增加一项声明，例如“本组织的会议应遵守《高效会议指南：1小时就能读懂的会议议事规则（第10版）》”。你还可以加上：“会员的日常会议应该由正式主持人主持，董事局的会议应该由非正式主持人主持。”同样，使用者可以对规则进行修改，让它们更加符合本组织的特殊需要。

客观裁判

这些规则是完整的。它们被采纳后，可以成为组织内部会议的正式议事规则。在需要的时候，这本书还可以成为议会成员或者裁判员。

支配要素

善政具有良好的机制。

政府管辖

一些有管辖权的政府机构要求，注册协会的章程和法规要由其成员批准，并且要每年提交报告。

章程

章程是一份简短的文件，用以说明组织的名称和宗旨。修改章程需要提前通知，需要大多数人无记名投票（即该组织全体成员的 2/3 或 3/4），如果组织被合并，则需要政府批准。事实上，有些条款是无法修改的，因此某个组织可能需要通过解散、重组来改变这些条款。

如今，许多非法人组织是在没有章程的情况下成立的，但也将所有管理规则写入规章中。

规章制度

一个组织的管理规则，涵盖会员制、官员、选举、职责、财务、会议、法定人数、纪律、修正案、印章管理等主题。修改需要提前通知，以获大多数无记名投票票数（即该组织全体成员的 2/3 或 3/4）或者政府批准的方式通过。

常设规则

常设规则是以往决策的记录，为未来提供指导，一般以清单的形式列出。常设规则可以在任何例会上进行修改，只要符合法定人数（要求出席成员的最少人数）且赞成票占大多数即可。

除非所有成员都在场，且没有异议，否则对现有的常设规则进行修改只适用于以后的会议。一些组织要求提前通知，才能对常设规则中列出的决定进行修改。

议事规则

一套议事规则是根据常设规则或内部规章制度建立的，并且各位成员同意根据这套规则管理他们的会议。这本书提供了一套完整的规则，可以用于任何组织团体。议事规则必须服从当地法律、法规，以及所有我们在本书中称为“法律 / 法则”的规则。

执行委员会

执行委员会是指在限定时间内选出的一组成员，他们根据各位成员的意愿，处理本组织的事务。他们的责任和权限在章程中有明确的规定，其权力要服从董事会。任何一名单独成员都不能承担任何特殊的权限和责任，除非董事会把上述权限授权给该成员。当一名成员承担了“董事”“管理委员会成员”“受托人”或“主管官员”的职责时，此人有义务完全按照各位成员的意愿行事。

高级职员

高级职员是指一些在限定时间内由各位成

员选出，或者由执行委员会任命的总裁、副总裁、秘书、司库等（他们的任期有一定的时限）。他们的责任和权限在章程中有规定。在有些组织中，这些高级职员组成了部分或整个执行董事会。

选举程序

选举程序通常载于章程中，规定何时举办选举、任职的要求和任期、提名和投票程序、投票方式以及计票人员的数量和任命。

做出决定的成员

当每个人都知道规则时，就比较容易做出好的决定。

最终决定权

只要与会人员达到规定人数，且会议和投票形式符合规章制度，会议上大多数在场成员的意愿即可形成最终决定，不能受到任何个人或预先决定的阻挠，除非有高一层的法律做出例外规定。

平等权利

除非另有规定，每个成员都有一次投票权，且在所有决定中享有同等的话语权。

主持人

由所有成员选出的某个人或者由委员会任命的人物，以确保会议顺利进行。

主持人的权力

主持人的职责是通过遵守规章制度和议事规则来保持会议的有序和公正。各成员必须听从主持人的领导，除非因会议程序问题进行投票表决，否则不允许进行讨论。

正式会议的主持人

在大型会议中，主持人必须（并且必须以可见方式）绝对不偏不倚。主持人必须避免用语言、姿态表达个人观点，并且不能参与到讨论中，除非以保持秩序的方式来引导会议。除极个别情况外，主持人获得了相关的简短信息，这时主持人可能会偏离中立规则，但是在绝大多数情况下，必须持不偏不倚的态度。主持人不能擅自提议。

如果主持人需要积极参与到讨论中，那么就需要安排其他成员来担任此项工作，直到对议案完成投票为止。任何成员都可以指出主持人在参与议事中出现的错误，主持人必须虚心接受。

非正式会议的主持人

在较小或非正式会议上，各位成员需要遵守规章制度、常设规则和习惯，主持人可以拥有和其他成员相同的权利，参与到讨论中。

向主持人申请发言

各位成员必须经过主持人的许可（口头或非口头的表态），才可以开始发言。如果几位成员同时站起来，主持人需要选择一个人先发言，并说明谁是下一个；其他人应该先坐下，等待发言者说完。在大型集会上，主持人需要安排各位成员按顺序发言，并把他们的名字记在一个清单上。最好让所有人都看到记录发言者顺序的清单，这通常很有用，尤其对虚拟会议来说。

法定人数

根据法律规定，会议做决定之前需要出

席会议的最少成员人数就是法定人数。主持人必须在确认达到法定人数的成员均已出席后，才能宣布会议开始。如与会人数减少，可能导致少于法定出席人数的情况，因此主持人必须随时知晓人员到会情况，并及时提醒各位成员。如果没有达到法定出席人数，会议只能以非正式形式开始；如果可能，应该当场召集其他相关人员使参会人数达到法定人数，或者确定召开下一次会议的时间。

会议议程

指在会议上讨论的事项和顺序，一般由秘书组织，提请执行委员会批准。在小型会议上，会议议程由主持人编写即可。会议议程应该提前通知所有成员。对虚拟会议来说，提前分发会议议程尤其重要。除非提出了另外的议案（需要由所有成员提供），否则议程可以由各位成员在会议过程中的任何时间进行修改。如果有一名或多名成员反对修改，就必须对会议议程的修改进行投票表决。会议议程应该包括：

- 宣布会议开幕，通过议程；

- 宣读往期会议的会议纪要；
- 宣读信函和报告；
- 讨论会议纪要、信函、报告中提出的业务；
- 讨论需要提交的议案及新的业务；
- 宣读通知；
- 宣布休会和会议结束时间。

议案和决定

有时，决定是通过全体成员达成共识做出的。此时，主持人会说：“如果没有人反对，那么……”主持人便陈述决定。有时，决定是通过议案和决议做出的。此时，其中一名成员会宣布：“我提议‘可以采取某些议案了’。”在想要提出任何议案前，必须有其他成员支持，以避免把时间花在讨论一个通过概率很低的想法上。

新的议案只有在待定议案被撤销或投票通过后才可以提出，否则会直接影响待定议案。影响待定议案的行为可能包括：

- 对议案的修改；
- 推迟到后续日期；
- 诉诸其他单位；

· 对发言者的时间进行规定；
· 对投票流程进行修改；
· 发生程序问题。

除非法律另有规定，否则成员在做出议案时必须在场，这样才能保护议案推动者的权益。如果已经就提出的议案向各位成员发出了通知，那么在议程上，任何出席成员都可以进行动议。

如果议案是清楚的，与任何法律不产生冲突，并且被附议，主持人或秘书应该将该议案宣读，并保证其被正确记录。有经验的提议者有时可以将书面的议案交给秘书。如果可能的话，该议案应该被正式宣读。

通常，允许提议者先提出议案，然后在讨论结束后再总结议案。

动议通知书

根据在后续会议中会进行的议案，动议通知书可以在会议中以口头或书面的方式发给各位成员。

特别会议

除非法律另有规定，否则出席特别会议的

成员只可以在会议上表决召开会议通知中规定的议题。

民意测试（测验民意的投票）

如果各位成员愿意，主持人可以在会议期间的任意时间举办一场无约束力的投票（测验民意的投票）。如果有成员反对，主持人应该询问各位成员的意见，并根据各位成员的投票决定是否举行民意投票。

提议者权益

在讨论中，可能会产生改进议案的想法。如果有成员反对，只要是在议案投票前，提议者可以在任意时间重新表述或撤回议案。如果重新表述或撤回议案需要有附议者，那么通过会议的帮助可以连续重新表述，直到议案与提议者希望的一样为止。

一旦提议者决定重新表述议案，或者议案通过了附议，那么该议案立刻会变为新的待定议案，并代替原有的议案，主持人或秘书可以宣读重新表述的议案。如果在宣读重新表述的议案前，有两名以上成员反对该议案，那么就只能通过另一个议案的方式对其进行修正。

修正案

如果由于反对，提议者没能或者不能对议案进行应有的更正，那么任何成员都可以根据原来的决议提出修正案。修正案可以通过删除、替换、增加文字来修改原来的议案，但是不能否定它或者改变其意图。

修正案被主持人批准或者被附议后，立刻可以变成新的待定议案，并且可暂时替代原来的议案。修正案对修正案的提议者给予原提议者相同的权利。前提是不改变其主题的重新表述，且必须经过主持人批准。提议修正案的细节将被讨论（不是原来的动议），接下来修正案将接受投票。除非一个修正案被另一个修正案击败或取代，否则不能被再次修正。

如果修正案获得通过，秘书应该宣读重新修改的议案。此时，这个新议案成为要经过讨论（如果有意愿）和投票的新的待定议案。它不可以根据提议者的权益重新表述、撤销，因为它原则上是由各位成员确立的，但是这个新的议案可以重新被批准、废除和修正。

如果修正案没有通过，那么原来的议案就重新变为待定议案。如果这份原来的议案就是原始议案（从来没有被修改过），那么原始的提议者会重新获得提议者的权益，可以对其进行进一步的修正，每次可以进行一项修改。

推迟、转交

在议案经过投票之前，任何一名成员可以在任意时刻，提出推迟待定议案（包括已经通过的修正案）到未来的某个不定或特定时刻再投票，或者转交给常务委员会，或者转交给特设的专门委员会，进行进一步研究。

任何相信对特别议案进行审议是不明智的成员，都可以提出“我们可以将议案推迟到某个时刻”。如果要推迟的议案获得附议或通过，那么这个特别议案不能在会上进一步讨论，但可以在另一场会上提出。议案不能被永久推迟，因为一场会议不能约束未来的会议。

投票

当所有希望发言的成员都完成了发言，主持人可以提议投票。除非某项议案需要多数票表决，否则满足法定人数并且有超过半数的赞成票即表示该议案已获得通过。废票和没有投票的成员不计数。

提议投票

认为讨论已经完成的成员可以呼吁，“我们准备好投票了”，或者由主持人提问，“你们准备好投票了吗”。回答只对主持人有指导意义，不能强制投票。认为主持人提出投票为时尚早的成员，或者认为投票推迟太久的成员，可以提出议事程序问题，并提议，“我们推迟投票进行进一步讨论”，或者“我们现在需要投票”。这样的提议需要附议，需要较少甚至不需要讨论即可进行投票。

各位成员的发言权利

每位成员有权对议案进行一次发言，但在大型会议上，需要通过议案来限定发言人的发言时间。如果还有没有发言的成员等待发言，主持人一般不应该接受“现在就投票”的提议。然而，如果问题双方的论点已经被公平提出，而且双方是在重复讨论，已经损害了良好的会议秩序，那么，主持人就可以接受这样的提议。

无论是通过一致同意的建议还是通过投票获得通过的建议，在各位成员决定投票后，主持人或秘书应该重新宣读一遍议案，保证所有成员都能理解这份议案。然后，主持人可以说，

“所有赞成议案的人请说‘赞同’（或者举手），所有反对的人请说‘反对’（或者举手）”，或者“现在请写下你们的选票”，等等，再开始投票。主持人必须宣布投票结果。如果需要计票，那么计票完成后由主持人宣布投票结果。

投票如何进行

一般习惯或常规法则决定了投票如何进行。一些团体通过声音投票，这样很难分辨其他人投的是什么票；一些团体通过举手、投票卡、起立、匿名、列队点名等方式进行投票，这使计票更加容易。如果主持人在秘书的协助下，不确定投票结果，主持人可以要求大家举手示意。如果仍然不清楚，主持人可以要求起立投票，并说：“请赞同的人起立，请就座；凡是反对的人，请起立，请就座。”

在必要情况下，任何认为有计票错误的成员都可以提出：“我们通过起立（或者投票）的方式重新进行计票。”如果这个议案获得附议并通过，那么就需要重新进行投票。可以提议要求通过投票方式表决，并且销毁记过的选票，然后宣布赞成票数和反对票数，或者采取与投票有关的其他措施。

缺席者投票

除非法律另有规定，允许代理人或缺席者投票，否则每一名成员都必须到场投票，无论是本人到场还是通过虚拟会议的方式出席。

道德观

每一名从决定中受益的成员都可以参与讨论，但是应该自觉退出投票。

投票平局

投票平局意味着议案没有通过。各位成员应该立即或者在未来的时间里重新思考该议案。在一些组织中，现有的法律规定主持人可以进行额外投票，打破平局。

大多数赞成票

如果一个成员认为这个议案需要许多成员的强烈支持，那么可以这样总结议案：“这个议案需要 3/4（或者其他某种比例）赞成票来获得通过。”由于大多数成员可以很容易地通过修正案废除这条要求，因此，如果没有通过修正案取消这种限制，会议就有需要大多数赞成票的要求。有时候，法律已经规定了要求大多数赞成票的情况，比如某些财务问题、规章制度的修改及其他重要事项。

非正式讨论

有时候，在提出议案前，非正式地讨论一种想法是有益的。要允许这种讨论，任何一名成员都可以提出："我们非正式讨论'某个议题'几分钟吧。"这个议案需要附议，并且几乎需要马上进行投票。在讨论议题后，如果没有新的议案，就需要着手进行会议议程中的下一项。

撤销议案

除非法律另有规定，否则在不损害契约的情况下，废除（撤销）原来决定的议案只需要大多数赞成票即可通过，并且可在日程允许的时间内开展（一般在面对新业务或者源于议事程序对议程进行了修改时）。

重新审议

如果决定对原来的议案进行重新审议，那

么在任何新的业务会议上，或者当它被提上议程后（或者通过议事程序后），就可以在该决定被同意后马上开展，然后在进行少量或不进行讨论后立刻进行投票。如果需要重新审议的议案获得通过，则需要一名成员提议同一主题的原有议案或者替代议案，议案会被再次讨论和投票。此时，提议者的权益仍然有效。新的决定可代替原来的决定。只要各位成员愿意，议案可以随时被重新审议。一旦做出了重新审议的决定，直到处理完重新审议的议案前，不可进行新的业务。

会议纪要

会议纪要是会议的记录，由秘书保管。它们至少应该包括所有主要的提议和议案。秘书要保存一套包括会议纪要、报告、信函等的文件系统。

当之前的会议纪要传达给所有成员后，主持人应该询问大家是否有修正。在所有修正都完成后，主持人应该询问，“所有支持采纳所发（或宣读、修正）的会议纪要的成员，请说‘赞同’（或者举手）”，“所有反对者，请说‘反对’（或者举手）”。然后宣布决定。会议纪要一经采纳，便由主持人和秘书签字，将成为在法庭等场所被普遍接受的正式记录。

报告

董事会、委员会和个人经常在会上向各位成员提供建议或者其他信息。

当含有上述信息的报告在会上宣读的时候，不需要任何议案。然而，在一些团体中通常会最后宣布，“我提议这份报告按宣读的方式接受”。意思是各位成员已经理解了这份报告。

如果报告中包含建议，那么提出报告的人就应该建议，“这份报告以宣读的方式被采纳”。意思是各位成员同意采纳这份报告及其建议。当然，任何一位成员都可以提出修正案，将其从“采纳”的状态变成“接受”状态，这样各位成员就不会受到报告中的建议的约束。一般财务报告都会被直接接受，而不是采纳，因为各位成员的职位不允许他们核实报告的准确性。

批准一个原有的决定

如果做出了决定，有时因为时间紧迫，

超过了某个成员、委员会、会议当时的权限，那么这个决定就可以在后续的会议中被具有权限的各位成员审批或否决。这需要一名成员去提议审批该决定。一般来说，要审批决定的议案会很快被通过。然而，如果该议案没有被通过，则成为非信任投票。除非在高一层级的法律（例如法规）中另有规定，否则做出这个有异议的决定的成员或团体必须辞职，或者通过选举替换他们。

休会

如果法规或现行规则需要在一个特定时间休会，那么主持人应在休会时间临近时提醒各位成员，让他们提出议案并尽快完成议程，或者在允许的情况下，提出议案将会议延迟。如果会议不能被延长，主持人应该宣布会议在特定时间休会。否则，主持人可以说："由于业务已经完成，如果没有反对，现在休会。"或者说："由于业务已经完成，让我们休会吧，所有赞同的人，请说'赞同'，所有反对的人，请说'反对'。"如果议案通过，主持人应该说："现在休会。"

保持会议顺畅

建设性的会议需要良好的秩序。

紧扣主题

各位成员每次只能讨论一个主题或议案。如果违反了这一规定，主持人应该打断发言者，坚持让他遵守这项规定。如果产生了有价值但是离题的想法，可以使用所谓“停车场”的理念，即主持人或秘书记录下这些想法，以便日后在合适的时间拿出来进行讨论，或者作为新的议程项目在未来重新开会讨论。

多想少说

每一位成员的讨论时间不能违背公平的原则，就一个议案的发言不能超过一次，直到其他人都完成了他们的发言轮次。不过，当出现新信息，或者一系列问题和回答涉及有用的事实时，可以产生例外。如果有必要，各位成员可以通过议案或建立常规规则，从下一场会议开始，限制每位发言者的时间，并指定一位计时员来强制要求该议案。

互相尊重

每位成员都必须尊重其他成员对议题拥有独立判断的权利。决定应该基于对事实的考虑，而不是发言者的技巧或者一个人对其他人应该如何投票的意见。每位成员的发言应该只能贡献光，而不是热！

禁止各位成员使用任何形式的个人批评、嘲讽带偏意见。每一位成员可以批评一种想法，但永远不要批评其他成员。除非会议程序允许，每一位成员都不能妨碍、干涉其他成员的发言。主持人应该坚持执行这项规定。

对会议程序有异议

每一位认为法律或会议的良好秩序已经被破坏的成员，都可以在任何时间起立并发言：

“主持人先生 / 女士，我对会议程序有异议。”主持人应该马上同意这位成员的申请，这位成员应简要解释为什么他 / 她觉得会议的规则、良好秩序被破坏了。

然后，主持人要规范这种程序，或者纠正现状或者解释为什么现状符合程序。

如果主持人宣布现状符合程序，这位成员可以行使最后的选择，提出说明：“主持人先生 / 女士，我申请对会议程序进行投票。”这位成员和主持人需要先后简要解释原因。然后在几乎没有进一步讨论的情况下，主持人需要主持投票并说明：“所有认为（这个行为）符合我们的程序（或良好的秩序）的人，请说‘赞同’（或举手示意）”，凡是不同意的人，请说‘否决’（或举手示意）。”主持人和这位提出程序问题的成员必须遵循这次投票。

干扰

不能容忍扰乱秩序者（通过延长发言故意拖延会议进程的人）或者通过任何其他行为干扰会议良好秩序的人。如果一位成员的发言时间过长，主持人应该对其进行礼貌的提醒。如果这位成员仍然继续，主持人可以打断他并在会上要求表决："我要求在会上进行表决，所有希望这位成员现在停止发言的人，请说'同意'（或举手）；所有反对的人，请说'否决'（或举手）。"如果表决结果是要求这位成员停止发言，那么主持人就可以说："先生/女士，各位成员要求你现在停止发言。请照做。"如果表决结果是"否决"，那么主持人就可以说："先生/女士，各位成员愿意让你继续。请照做。"

如果一位成员或多位成员在主持人要求后，或者议案已经被各位成员通过后，仍然不停止发言，则主持人可以将其打断，或者发起动议要求该成员离开会场。如果有必要，还可以发起动议要求休会，待日后重新召开，但这样的决定只有其他成员可以做出。不应该对任何一位成员使用身体强制措施，但可以根据主持人的需要，撤掉发言者的麦克风。

不同观点

如果各位成员对法规或流程等的含义存在不同观点，主持人可以协调解决争端。例如，主持人可以提出一个用来解决争端的提案，并要求大家举手表决。

最终的决定取决于各位成员。

新主持人

做主持人应该不是一项吓人的工作，本书中的规则已经很直白了，在必要情况下，你的同事也可以协助你。你应该表明你愿意接受帮助。如果你忘了某件事，就让他们提醒你。你可以这样建议："如果你们觉得我可以用更有效的方式主持会议，那么请让秘书给我一份议事手册，手册中有已经强调了的那些我需要审查的点。"

除了预先学习各项规章制度、常设法规及会议规则，学习日程也很有用。可以用备忘录记录下来，这样在开会的时候就不会忘记。顺便说一下，准时开始会议是一个好习惯。

委员会和小型会议

非正式会议也可以有良好的秩序。

委员会

委员会是指由董事会或各位成员任命的由一名或多名成员组成的一组人，负责担任一项长期或短期的职务。常务委员会是长期的，直到解散为止，其成员可以定期更换。临时委员会是为负责某项特定任务而临时组建的。委员会主持人由各位成员选举产生，或者由董事会指定。除非另有说明，委员会或会议的法定人数都是成员的大多数。一般使用书面指南保证其工作秩序和连续性。

非正式会议

在委员会和一些小型会议中，主持人可以作为领导非正式地参与进来——但要服从法律和会议的意图，因此也要对任命机构本身负责。按照会议正式程度递增的顺序，下面是会议类型的举例清单：

· 由主持人领导的工作组一致同意后做出决定。

· 小型会议根据一致同意做出较小的决定，由主持人宣布，并记录在会议纪要中。

· 有议程和议案执行的委员会会议，由主持人附议、表决、宣布，并由秘书记录在会议记录中。

特别委员会

大多数委员会是民主的，但在一些非民主的委员会中，尽管其他人可以帮忙，但是只有一个人负有全部责任。

作为一个委员会会议的主持人

在理想情况下，委员会会提出一个融合了多人经验和智慧的主题。但有时候，善意的人会发言太多，或者用力过盛，意识不到这种行为浪费了多少时间，以及对他人是多么不公平。会议必须避免这样的不平衡。主持人不应容许任何成员过度支配会议。

主持人应该协助各位成员专注于手头上的议案（社交活动可以在会议之前或之后进行）。轻度幽默是必要的，但是要简洁。应该控制不同意见的答复，不要让其成为一个论点。应该让事实说话。会议应保持安静，让成员们可以思考。这通常是有效组织的标志。

当需要把一种想法记录下来，或者写成信函的时候，大多数委员会同意最好由一名或两名人员进行书写、修改，然后提交到整个委员会进行最终审议。

在各种规格的会议中，最理想的是各位成员作为一个整体寻找最佳的解决方案，而不是各有各的想法并都希望自己的想法被采纳。（如果能实施到位，对于立法机构也一样！）

非民主会议

某些会议（例如经理给职员培训的销售会议）并不以民主决策为目标，但是尊重每个人、遵守本书中的基本原则，将可以提高会议效率。这一点同样适用于小型的民主决策。在可能的情况下，这样做一般都会给会议带来亮点，让所有与会者对会议更加感兴趣。

第二部分 进一步的帮助

常见问题

与主持人有关的问题

Q1. 主持人应该具备什么样的品质？

A1. 自我控制能力强，拥有良好的幽默感，对章程、规章制度、常设规则和组织秩序规则有充分的了解。

Q2. 为了保证有争端的议题得到公平、和谐地讨论，主持人可以做什么？

A2. 如果需要，主持人可以提醒各位成员：

· 在大家已经同意遵守的规则下讨论，即使在意见有强烈分歧的时候，也能以有序的方式，共同做出决定。

· 成员在讨论时有不被打断的权利，包括在发言的时候拥有不理会任何人的回应的自由。

· 已经发言过一次的成员，不管其他人的陈述多么过度，都不能立即回应其他成员的发言，要等到所有想要发言的人都完成发言才可以做出回应。

·每一位成员想要发言，都必须得到主持人的认可。

·成员不需要更改自己的观点，但作为有权限的决策者，必须接受大多数人的投票。

Q3. 主持人应该怎么样处理有对抗意图或者愤怒的成员？

A3. 最有效的方法是保持平静、客观、积极的态度，并提醒自己保持礼貌，不冲动，这样会有助于保持可控局势。同情不太能控制自己情感的人，会让主持人免于犯同样的错误。处理此类问题，有经验之后会容易很多。

Q4. 主持人可以投票吗？

A4. 可以，除非法律另有规定。然而，正式会议的主持人应该尽量不露声色地进行投票，以避免表现出自己的偏好。

Q5. 如果主持人和副主持人都缺席，应怎样召开会议？

A5. 任何成员，包括秘书，都可以召开会议、申请并举行这场会议的临时主持人选举。

Q6. 主持人是否应该引导会议讨论?

A6. 偶尔的口头总结很有用，但是参加正式会议的主持人必须小心，要保持不偏不倚。

让会议更有意义，保持会议的正常秩序，使过分热情的成员不至于主导会议，帮助各位成员每次清晰地表明一个观点，避免会议拖拉、重复，能够做到这些的主持人就算已经为会议做了很多贡献了。在主持人的领导下，较小的决定可以通过一致同意的方式做出。例如，主持人可以说："除非有反对意见，否则我们接下来的会议就不需要吵闹的麦克风了。"

与秘书有关的问题

Q7. 会议纪要应该多详细?

A7. 要像秘书及成员们期望的一样详细。会议纪要应包含通过的所有议案，以及对所有主要活动的简要介绍。会议纪要通常看起来像扩大的会议议程。正式会议的纪要一般比非正式会议的更加详细。非正式会议的纪要可以简单到带日期的各个活动、决定的清单。

Q8. 会议纪要必须包括提议者和附议者的名字吗?

A8. 不。但在更加正式的会议中，秘书应该加上他们的名字，或者各位成员可以通过议案要求加上。

Q9. 过往会议的会议纪要需要在会议开始前宣读吗?

A9. 不需要。如果会议纪要已经分发下去了（无论是会议前还是开始时），那么各位成员不需要再听别人大声宣读它。各位成员可决定会议议程。

Q10. 当过往会议的会议纪要被修改后，秘书是否需要重新编写?

A10. 一般来说，要在文本上或在秘书的会议纪要副本的文本或页边空白上进行修改，并由主持人和秘书签字。不过，如果秘书愿意或各位成员通过了这样的议案，那么会议纪要就需要重新编写，新的副本由主持人和秘书签字。虚拟会议可让主持人和秘书通过电子手段在会议纪要上签字，标明修改日期后进行分发。

Q11. 如果采纳了过往会议的会议纪要，之后发现其中有错误，应该怎么办?

A11. 一旦采纳和签署了会议纪要，被签字的版本就不能更改。应该标注修改之处，在之后的会议中由各位成员共同通过，并将其写入会议记录。应该将记录后续的修改附在原来的会议纪要上，标明日期，并由主持人和秘书签字。在虚拟会议中，任何修改的电子版会议纪要都应该标注修改日期。

Q12. 秘书是否可以发起议案？

A12. 除了正式会议的主持人，任何成员都可以发起议案。然而在大型会议中，议案通常是由全体成员发起的。

议案和其他话题

Q13. 在没有指定的推动者时，可以将议案提上日程吗？

A13. 可以。任何成员都可以提议把议案提上日程。如果议案没有提议成功，就进行议程上的下一个项目。

Q14. 提议者的权利有哪些？

A14. 当成员们互相合作时，提议者的权利可以让他们以简单、自然的方式改善议案。经验越多，效率越高。如果有两名以上的成员反对，就需要更加正式的修正流程，所以这项权利不可以被滥用。

Q15. 一名成员可以投票否决自己的议案吗？

A15. 可以。对各位成员唯一的限制都在“保持会议顺畅”部分标明了。然而，如果使用提议者权益修改议案或推出修订案，可能会更加明智。

Q16. 一名缺席的成员可以针对议程上的议案提交一份书面的修订案吗？

A16. 不可以，除非更高层级的法律另行规定。不过，这位成员可以在议程上增加一个议案来说明问题。这个议案需要在将要进行的会议中提议和附议。在虚拟会议中，提议和附议可以通过电子形式进行。缺席的成员有被告知会议纪要中决定的权利。

Q17. 各位成员可以在会议中增加、修改常设规则，从而给主持人制造平局投票吗？

A17. 不能。他们可以修改常设规则，但因为会议受到现有的常设规则约束，所以修改后的常设规则要在下次会议才能生效。这项规则保护了没有出席特别会议的各位成员的权利：在缺少他们参与决策的情况下，其他人是不能修改会议中的主要规则的。然而，如果所有的成员出席会议，且没有异议，那就可以马上修改常设规则。

Q18. 如我们的法定人数是 40 人，且 40 位成员都出席会议。在投票中，有 8 人投赞同票，7 人投反对票，还有 1 张废票，即不赞同也不反对，其余 24 位成员没有投票，那么这项议案通过了吗？

A18. 是的。议案通过有两个必要条件：出席的成员总人数必须达到法定人数；大多数的法定投票都是赞同票。

在这个案例中，两项条件都符合。废票和没有投票的不计入在内。8 票是 15 票法定投票中的大多数。

Q19. 如果某位成员需要中场休息应该怎么办？

A19. 这位成员可以提出会议程序问题，并提议各位成员休息一下，然后在规定的时间重新开会。

Q20. 在会议中可以修改日程，从而纳入早已经考虑过的特定话题吗？

A20. 可以。在适宜的时间，某名成员可以对程序提出异议（假定提出的修改将改善会议的良好秩序），并在日程中提议修改。

Q21. 什么时候可以重新开始讨论被无限期推迟的议案？

A21. 在未来的会议中，在议程允许的时间（一般在出现了新的业务或者源于程序问题修改日程时）。

Q22. 如法规规定，在会议上，任何花费超过1000美元的议案都需要提交动议通知。比如，有个预知议案是要安装一个5000美元的电子安全系统，已经将其提前发给了所有成员。在会议中，这项议案被修改了，改为决定采购更好的、售价仅为4000美元的锁具。这样可以接受吗？

A22. 可以。这个金额在预知议案规定的财政限度内，并且议案也同样是关于安全话题的。如果在话题上存在差异，那么主持人就应该询问："你们同意我采纳这个符合预知议案话题的议案吗？如果同意，请举手，如果反对，请举手。”由此强调各位成员拥有最终决定权。

然而，（通过行使提议者权利或者一个修正案的方式）将议案改变为购买一个5200美元的安全系统将不会被接受，因为这个额度超过了预知议案确立的界限。同理，变更议案为购买一个5000元的音响系统也不会被接受，因为主题不一样了。

Q23. 我们如何才能召开一个轻松、互动的“智库”会议，以有序的方式和最大的自由度探索解决问题的新方法?

A23. 使用非正式讨论规则解除会议中的各种“清规戒律”。然后任命一位主持人或一位成员担任中立的提议者，保证在完全没有预先立场的情况下，每种想法都能被接受，这样就不会有人提出“异想天开”的想法了。此外，还应该任命一位秘书或一位成员作为记录员，在黑板上列出所有想法、图表，以保证它们不会被忘记。

大型会议有时候会分解为若干个小型会议，其中，每个小型会议都有各自的提议者和记录员。当会议结束时，各个团队聚集在一起倾听提议者的报告。这些会议上的想法可能会产生议案。

Q24. 可以举例说明什么是可接受的和不可接受的修正案吗?

A24. 考虑下这个议案："我建议我们下次去山姆饭馆。"

修正案 1："我建议修正这个议案，把'山姆'这个词用'金塔'代替。"这是可接受的，因为他没有否决议案或改变主题。

修正案 2："我建议修正这个议案，在'去'这个字前面添加'不'这个字。"这是不可接受的，因为它否决了原有的议案。通过推翻原有的议案可以更容易地获得同样的结果。

Q25. 什么叫作点名投票?

A25. 由秘书叫出每位成员的名字，然后被叫人进行口头投票，并将每位成员的投票记录在一份清单上。

Q26. 什么叫作决议?

A26. 决议是对会议在某个话题上的意见的正式表达，或者是决定采取某种行动的一种特别的说法。它通常包含一个或多个前提的开场白，然后得出结论。例如："我建议我们采用以下决议：当在（一个或多个前提）的情况下，解决方法是（解决方法）。"当然，在对整个议案进行投票前，各位成员可以通过行使提议者权利或提交修正案改变决议的任何部分。

Q27. 能否举例说明民意调查（民意投票）是什么样的?

A27. 当考虑采购一台新电脑时，有名成员希望了解有多少成员使用它，并请求主持人进行调查。主持人说："如果没有反对，我们对这个问题进行举手表决。如果我们采购一台电脑，有多少人会使用它?"然后主持人宣布结果。如果有一名成员反对这种民意调查，主持人应该询问："所有希望本次会议进行这项民意调查的，请说'赞同'；所有反对的，请说'反对'。"主持人应根据会议的结果决定是否进行民意调查。

Q28. 你能否给出一个高层级的法律如何修改议事规则的例子?

A28. 在平等权利法则下，每名成员可以且只可以投出一票。然而，在一些辖区，管辖社区业主会议的法律规定，同一业主拥有的每个公寓单元都拥有一票。一名拥有五个公寓单元的业主就有五票。类似的，在一家公司的股东会议上，投票数一般与股东持有的股份数量成正比。

另一个例子是关于投票平局的规则。在一些管辖区，比如，在一些有关公寓业主的法规中，法律规定除了主持人原有的一票，会议还可以再给主持人一张票，以打破平局。

Q29. 我们的董事会花了 7000 美元用来维修电梯，并称这属于“紧急事务”，但预算上限是 2000 美元。这种行为是否合规？

A29. 是的。在下一次常规或特别会议上，各位成员必须批准这项预算。一般这项议案都会获得通过。如果批准预算的议案没有通过，那么各位成员将会对董事会失去信任，必须举行选举，对其成员进行替换。

Q30. 这些规则适用于大会、讲座和立法会议吗？

A30. 是的，这些规则与议程、代表、发言顺序和限制、投票方式，以及与这些事件顺利操作的诸多细节有关的特别流程和规则相结合，效果会很好。

要修改这些议事规则，用常设规则和规章制度使他们符合特殊需求，是很容易的。

Q31. 正式主持人可以在会议中提出议案吗?

A31. 如果主持人自己不想参与，可以安排另外一位成员提出议案。主持人也可以作为普通成员参与，可以要求副主持人、秘书或另一名成员在自己所提出的议案进行讨论、投票过程中，主持会议。

Q32. 如果成员发现主持人或委员会有偏见，应该怎么办?

A32. 任何一名成员都可以对议事程序提出异议，坚持让主持人（或委员会）遵守双方对某一事项讨论的公平性。如果有正式主持人，各位成员应坚持让主持人不偏不倚。

会议示范

以下是根据书中的规则做的会议示范。这是一个包含如何利用这些规则应对难堪处境的虚拟会议。在阅读之前，我们建议你首先透彻阅读第一部分的规则和常见问题，了解这些是普遍常识的规则。如此，这个会议示范才会更有用。

C= 主持人

M= 成员

C：欢迎！让我们开会吧。议程有任何更改吗？ M1？

M1：我建议从议程中删除关于鱼塘的建议。

M2：我附议这个议案。

C：这个议案成立且被附议，要求从议程中删除关于鱼塘的提议。

[讨论]

C：你们准备好进行投票了吗？

[所有成员都说，“我们现在投票吧”]

C：既然你们准备好投票了，请秘书宣读议案。

[秘书宣读议案]

C：所有赞成把鱼塘问题从议程中删除的，请举手……所有反对的，请举手……谢谢。投票平局。

有40张赞同票和40张反对票，因此议案没有通过，议程保持不变。我们上一次会议的会议纪要已经分发。有需要更改和遗漏的地方吗？有吗，M3？

M3：会议是从下午7：30开始，而不是从下午8：00开始。

C：谢谢你M3。如果没有任何反对，请秘书现在进行更正。还有其他要更正的吗？……所有赞成会议纪要更正的人，请举手……所有反对的人，请举手……谢谢你们。会议纪要的更正已被采纳，秘书和我现在在上面签字。

C：议程中的下一个事项是一份董事局的报告，由 M4 宣读。

[M4 宣读报告]

M4：我建议这份报告按所宣读的予以采纳。

M5：我附议这个议案。

C：M4 提出报告按照所宣读的予以采纳，并得到附议，M6？

M6：我认为我们不应该按照这份报告的建议更改我们的管理公司。我建议 M4 把“采纳”一词改为“接纳”。

C：M4，你同意进行这个修改吗？

M4：不，我不希望进行这个修改。

C：所以呢，M6？

M6：那我提议修改这个议案，把“采纳”一词改为“接纳”。

M7：我附议这个议案。

C：这个议案获得提议、附议，要求我们修改议案，把“采纳”一词改为“接纳”，从而让各位成员不必按照报告中的建议执行。

[讨论]

［各位成员称，“让我们现在投票吧！”］

C：如果没有任何反对，我们现在就投票。所有赞成对议案进行修改，把“采纳”一词改为“接纳”的人，请举手……所有反对的人，请举手……谢谢你们。修正案没有通过，现在我们必须考虑采用原本议案，不做更改。还有要进一步讨论的吗？如果没有，我们现在进行投票。所有支持采用所宣读的这份报告的人，请举手……所有反对的人，请举手……谢谢。这个议案通过。

M8：主持人，我对程序问题提出异议。

C：怎么了，M8？

M8：两次投票太靠近了。我建议我们重新进行投票。

C：我对投票结果满意。M8 你呢？

M8：嗯，我不满意，我提议我们重新进行投票！

M9：我附议这个议案。

C：所有赞同重新进行投票的人，请起立并保持站立，直到我说“谢谢”。请秘书帮我计算下人数好吗？……谢谢。所有反对的人，请起立。秘书，请再帮我计算下人数……谢谢。37 票赞同，43 票反对，重新利用选票进行投票的议案没有通过。因此，原来的议案中采用 M4 报告中的建议获得通过。议程上的下一个事项是关于鱼塘的，M10？

M10：我提议，现在对鱼塘的想法进行几分钟的非正式讨论。

M11：我附议这个议案。

C：现在所有赞同以非正式方式讨论鱼塘的人请举手……所有反对的人请举手……谢谢。这个议案获得通过，所以我们现在以非正式方式讨论这个话题。

[非正式讨论]

M12：由于我们还没准备好对这个问题提出议案，我提议我们现在继续下面的议程。

M13：我附议这个议案。

C：所有赞同现在继续下一个议程的人，请举手……所有反对的人，请举手……谢谢。这个议案获得通过。会议纪要中提到的下一个事项，是我们上次开会中提出的对大楼进行粉刷的议案，M14？

M14：由于我相信这个议案应得到大多数成员的支持，所以其中包含了特别要求。我建议我们把大楼外部的所有木料进行粉刷，总预算不超过 20000 美元，这个议案需要 75% 的赞成票才能通过。

M15：我附议这个议案。

C：由于各位成员已经获得通知，这个议案符合我们的法规。请秘书宣读一下。

[秘书宣读议案]

C：M14，你要针对你的议案发言吗？

[M14 对议案进行发言]

[讨论]

M14：在倾听讨论后，我希望把我的议案重新组织并宣读如下：我们把大楼的外窗框进行粉刷，总预算不超过 10000 美元，同时这个预案需要 75% 的赞同票才能通过。

M16：我附议这个议案。

M17：我反对在议案中进行这个修改。

M18：我也反对在议案中修改。

C：由于有两人反对，这个议案不能根据提议者权益进行修改，原本的议案仍然作为待定议案进行讨论，M14？

M14：我提议把议案中的“大楼外部的所

有木料”的字句，改为“大楼的外窗框”，并且把价格从“20000美元”改为“10000美元”。

M19：我附议这个议案。

C：这个修正案合规。请秘书宣读修正案，保证它的正确性。

[秘书宣读修正案]

C：这个修正案的提议者可以首先发言。

[讨论]

[各位成员呼吁，“我们现在投票吧！”]

C：没有听到反对意见，我们现在投票吧。请秘书宣读修正案。

[秘书宣读修正案]

C：所有赞同这个修正案的人，请举手……所有反对的人，请举手……谢谢。大多数人赞同，修正案通过。新修正的议案现在成为待定议案。请秘书宣读这个新议案。

[秘书宣读议案]

[讨论]

C：还有进一步讨论吗？请秘书再次宣读新的议案，然后我们进行投票。

[秘书宣读议案]

C：是否所有人都理解了我们投票的内容？……为了让计票更加容易，我们采用起立方式投票。所有赞同议案的人，请起立……所有反对的人，请起立……谢谢。

有 48 票赞同，32 票否决，表示其中 60% 为赞同票。议案要求 75% 的赞同票才能获得通过。议案没有通过，M20？

M20：我提议我们重新考虑这个议案。

M21：我附议这个议案。

C：所有赞同重新考虑这个议案的人，请举手……所有反对的人，请举手……大多数赞同，要重新考虑的议案获得通过，M22？

M22：可进行细微修改，我想这种想法会获得通过。我建议我们把大楼外窗刷漆，预算不超过 15000 美元，这个议案需要 75% 的赞同票才能获得通过。

M23：我附议这个议案。

C：请秘书宣读这个议案。

[秘书宣读议案]

[讨论]

C：M24？

M24：主持人，我建议现在投票。

M25：我附议这个议案。

C：等轮到发言的 M26 结束发言，我会接受你的议案。

M26：谢谢。

[M26 发言]

C：现在投票的议案已经被提出并得到附议，我们现在进行投票。

M28：主持人，我对程序问题提出异议。我们中有几个人想对这个议案发言。

C：问题的双方都已经在过去 20 分钟内公平发言了。有超过 80 名成员在场。我们让各位成员决定。

所有赞同现在投票的人，请举手……所有

反对的人，请举手……谢谢。议案继续，我们现在投票。秘书，请再次宣读议案。

[秘书宣读议案]

C：谢谢。我们采用起立方式投票。所有赞同的人，请起立……谢谢。所有反对的人，请起立……谢谢。60 票赞成票对 20 票反对票，赞成票达到总票数的 75%，因此议案通过。董事会现在可以着手这项工作。我们下一个议程是新议案，M29？

M29：我建议我们重新考虑这个议案。

M30：我附议这个议案。

C：所有赞同重新考虑最后这个议案的人，请举手……所有反对的人，请举手……需要重新考虑议案的建议被否决了。

M30：我提议重新考虑上一个议案。

M29：我附议这个议案。

C：这个议案已经在程序之外，我们已经对其做出了决定，M30？

M30：主持人，它还没有在程序之外。《高效会议指南：1 小时就能读懂的会议议事规则（第 10 版）》中提到，“只要各位成员愿意，就可以重新考虑一个议案”。

C：各位成员已经决定了他们不愿意重新考虑这个议案，所以我们现在讨论新议案，M31？

M31：我的公寓就在游戏室隔壁，玩家经常很吵。我提议这个游戏室每天晚上 9：00 关闭。

C：有没有对这个议案的附议者？

这个议案由于缺乏附议者，失败。

M32：我提议我们在游戏室贴一个标语，要求玩家晚上 9：00 以后保持安静。

M33：我附议这个议案。

C：在游戏室贴一个标语要求玩家晚上 9：00 以后保持安静的议案得到提议和附议。有没有讨论？

M34：议案中需要说明这个标语预算的上限。

C：M32？

M32：好主意。我希望改变我的宣读议案，要求置办委员会花费不到 45 美元，在游戏室贴一个标语，要求玩家晚上 9：00 以后保持安静。

M33：我附议这个新的议案。

M35：我反对对 M32 的原来议案进行这个修改。

C：由于只有 1 人反对，因此这项修改是可以被接受的。请秘书宣读新的议案。

[秘书宣读议案]

C：M36？

M36：由于有其他因素需要考虑，我提议我们把这个议案交给董事会，让他们考虑，要求他们在下次会议中向我们报告。

M37：我附议这个议案。

[讨论]

C：还有其他人吗？……我们把这个议案交给董事会，让他们考虑，要求他们在下次会议中向我们报告，这已得到提议和附议。所有赞同的人，请举手……所有反对的人，请举手……议案通过。还有其他的新议案吗？ M38？

M38：三次会议之前我们决定了给门厅铺地毯，但现在还什么都没做。我提议我们废除给门厅铺地毯的议案！

M34：我附议这个议案。

M39：主持人，我对程序问题提出异议。

C：M39，请讲。

M39：合同已经交给一家公司，根据我们的议事规则，我们不能废除这个议案。

C：我相信你是对的，M39。如果废除会

违反合同，我们不能废除这个议案。M38？

M38：颜色错了！价格太高了！我们并没有违反合同！合同还没有签！我坚持我们……

M39：我同意……

C：稍等一下。M39！请等到允许你发言时再发言。

M38：主持人，我对程序问题提出异议。

C：请讲，M38。

M38：我相信这个议案合规，并要求对程序问题进行投票。

C：谢谢你，M38。请解释你的理由。然后，我会解释我的理由，接着我们将进行投票。

[M38 解释]

[C 答复]

C：现在由各位成员进行表决。所有认为废除这个议案是违规的人，请举手……所有反对的人，请举手……谢谢。议案通过。要废除原有议案的议案违规，我们现在着手进行下一个议案。

[讨论更多的业务]

C：常设规则要求我们晚上 10：00 休会。现在只剩下 10 分钟了。M40？

M40：我提议我们把常设规则改为，“我们在晚上 10：00 休会，如果各位成员希望延后，可将休会延到稍后时间”。

M41：我附议这个议案。

C：由于我们受到现有的常设规则支配，这个议案如果通过，不影响今晚的结束时间。我们面前这个议案是把常设规则修改为“我们在晚上 10：00 休会，如果各位成员希望延后，可将休会延到稍后时间。”

[短暂讨论]

[各位成员呼吁投票]

C：请秘书宣读议案。

[秘书宣读议案]

如果没有反对，我们现在投票。所有赞同的人，请举手……所有反对的人，请举手……议案通过，各位成员可以在未来的会议中把休会时间延后了。现在晚上 10：00 了，我宣布这个会议休会！

会议议事规则流程图

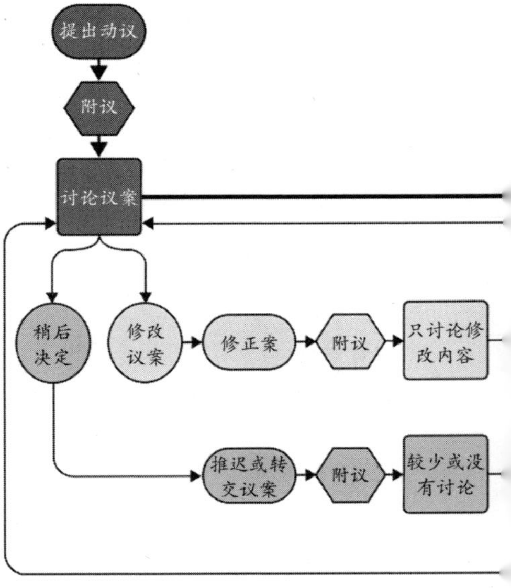

保持会议的良好秩序需做到以下几点：

· 会议紧扣议题；
· 每次由一个主持人认可的发言者发言；
· 发言时，他人不得干扰。

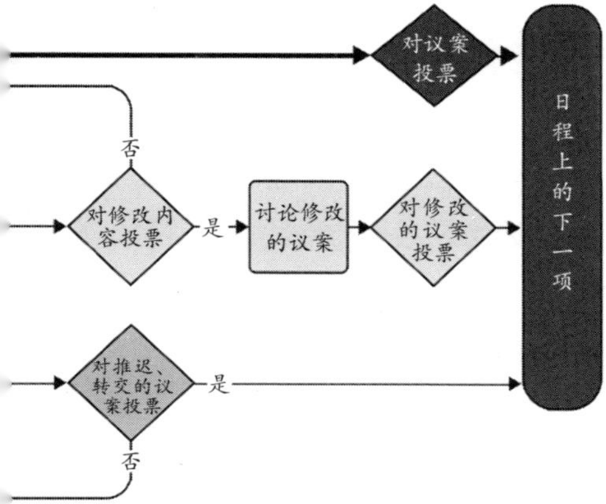

对程序提出异议的几个注意点

· 某一位成员解释如何做是违反某条法律或良好秩序的；

· 主持人对程序问题具有裁决权；

· 如果有必要则进行投票。

规则总结

公平性（各位成员的权利平等）和保持会议的良好秩序是基本原则。

只要出席人数达到法定人数，最终的决定权在于各位可投票成员中的大多数，同时一定要服从任何高一级的法律（当地法律、章程、规章制度、现有的常设规则等）。

在正式会议中，主持人应公正地主导会议，但不参与任何讨论。在非正式会议中，主持人可作为平等成员参与讨论。

议案应得到肯定表述，并且不得与高一级法律相抵触。任何议案都需要一名附议者。

只要存在一名附议者，同时不超过一名成

员反对，提议者权益允许提议者对议案进行重新表述或撤回。

修正案可以在待定议案中删除、替换、增加字句，但是不可以否决议案或者更改其主题。修正案不可以再被修正。

推迟、转交：议案可以无限期推迟到未来的某个具体场合讨论、投票，或转交给一个委员会进行进一步研究。

投票：普通投票包括以选票、起立、举手、投票卡和口头的方式进行的投票。要让议案获得通过，与会人数必须达到法定人数，且超过半数的投票必须为赞同票。

非正式讨论：以非正式的方式讨论某个话题的议案，如果获得通过，可允许各位成员在非正式的情况下考虑某种想法。

撤销、重新审议：各位成员可以在任何适当的时间，撤销或重新审议过往的决定。

批准一个原有的决定：如果一个决定超越

了某名成员的职权，委员会或会议可以在未来的会议中进行批准。

良好秩序：各位成员每次只讨论一个议题。除非会议程序允许，一位成员绝对不能占用超过公平限度的讨论时间，也不能打断其他成员的发言。

对会议程序有异议：每一名认为法律或良好秩序正在被破坏的成员，都可以马上起立并提出“对会议程序有异议”。主持人应允许该成员解释原因，如有必要，应呼吁就此投票表决。

附录：原文

Foreword

Fred and Peg Francis have done an amazing job. Their book is absolutely indispensable for anyone who conducts meetings or participates in democratic discussion at any level--from parliamentary assemblies to condominium annual meetings. What the Francises have succeeded in doing is cutting through the forbidding complexities of running a meeting and reducing them to a simple set of common-sense rules that anyone can follow. When this book is employed, the disappointments that accompany many meetings can be sharply reduced and democratic participation greatly improved.

Over the years, I have chaired or attended hundreds of meetings at the governmental, business, church, and social levels and have often been frustrated by the difficulties of properly presiding over such meetings so that everyone can understand the process, and the will of the majority can be formulated and prevail. Much of the difficulty arises from the fact that few have the time or inclination to study the old-style rule books, and are therefore easily intimidated--even tyrannized sometimes--by the very few who know them.

The Francises' book is making an important contribution to democracy. It can be readily adopted by any group, council, union, or corporation, and will be of lasting benefit. Speaking personally, I have sat through years of parliamentary debate and appreciate the value--and necessity--of achieving consensus in a democratic proceeding by having rules and following them. Up until now, the rules have been exceedingly complex, often confusing, and unsatisfactory at many levels. From here on in, those groups who adopt *Democratic Rules of Order* will find significant improvement in both the tenor of their meetings and the validity of the results.

Douglas Leiterman was Parliamentary
Correspondent for *Southam News*, an
Executive Producer at CBC, and CEO of
Motion Picture Bond Company

Preface

Are you frustrated by meetings that lack efficiency ... fail to move smoothly through an agenda ... lose order and professionalism due to emotional outbursts ... or do not foster constructive decision-making that truly represents the wishes of the membership?

You're not alone. And it doesn't have to be that way!

After years of volunteering their time for community groups--including attending hundreds of professional and nonprofit meetings--Fred and Peg Francis recognized the need for a concise, authoritative resource to assist boards of directors, committees, and other organized groups seeking to fairly represent their memberships by hosting efficient, effective meetings.

Because they could not find such a resource, they created one. It took several years of refining (and a great deal of input from executives, parliamentarians, and other users) to perfect the rules, to be sure that each point was crystal clear, and that not a single necessary rule was missing. Introduced in 1994 as

Distinctly Democratic Rules of Order (changed to *Democratic Rules of Order* in later printings), this easy-to-use book has become a respected and valued reference for thousands of organizations, large and small, and for students being taught the democratic process in classrooms around the world.

Used By Diverse Groups

From unions and professional associations to strata councils, churches, and nongovernmental organizations, *Democratic Rules of Order* is a "pocket guide" setting out a step-by-step process that allows all members to participate in the exchange of ideas and group decision-making, including virtual meetings.

The book can be read in less than an hour and is intentionally small, so it is easy to carry to meetings for on-the-spot reference when a question arises.

Easy-to-use Format

To make it easy to follow, the book is divided into two parts. *Part 1: The Rules* describes organizational structures and members' roles, and it includes step-by-step procedures for handling the most critical part of any meeting: the decision-making process. It helps the reader navigate through the democratic processes of:

- introducing ideas
- making motions and amendments
- handling points of order and disturbances
- managing the voting process
- working on and with committees

Part 2: Further Help provides additional important reference information, including:

- frequently asked questions
- a scripted example of a meeting that uses all the key elements of *Democratic Rules of Order*
- a flowchart that illustrates the rules of order
- a summary of the rules of order for quick reference during a meeting

Since 1996, this book has been a best seller in Canada. By reaching a wider audience with this 10th edition, the authors hope to improve the world, one meeting and one decision at a time.

PART 1 The Rules

Introduction

Fairness and Orderliness

These parliamentary rules of order help people to deliberate and consider ideas together,and then make decisions as wisely, fairly, and easily as possible. These rules are relevant for meetings of any size that are undivided by organized political parties. Ideally, decisions are based on objective consideration of facts, unaffected by emotions, group pressures, or unnecessary protocols. The purpose of this book is to help your organization reach this ideal.

Democratic Principles

This book is not an abridged version of other books. It is

a complete set of rules determined by common practice and the natural laws of democracy--"rule by the ruled," as Webster's dictionary puts it. These self-evident principles, when applied to decision-making meetings, include:

•the right of each individual member to participate equally and fully in orderly meetings that are free from intimidation, filibustering, and other disturbances and in which all members will follow the same easily understood rules, including the right to be equally and fully informed of all events, whether a member is present or not

•the right of the majority of members to make the decisions

A Democratic Ideal

We should remember that we all belong to the same organization, with a common purpose. We can have widely differing views and still work together for a common good without dividing into opposing sides, each trying to get its own way. The best decisions are made when we listen thoughtfully to the information being presented and then make our own decisions privately.

Another Democratic Ideal

Must we accept a legal decision if it is a bad one? Yes and

no. Yes, because, to practice democracy, we must accept the decision and do what it requires us to do. No, because we are not required to change our opinion. At some later date, the opportunity may occur for a review of the decision or we may even find that the decision was good after all!

Degrees of Formality

In small or close-knit groups, decisions can often be made by consensus or general agreement, provided that the chair or secretary recording each decision is sure that most members agree.

Large groups, too, often make decisions informally. The mover's privilege allows cooperative members to work out decisions quickly and easily. A more formal amending process is automatically required if opinions are divided. The degree of formality is usually determined by custom, agreement, or a law as defined in the next paragraph.

Higher Laws

Rules of order are automatically overruled when a law of the land, a constitution, a bylaw, or an existing standing rule applies. Throughout this book, we refer to any of these as a *law*.

Rules of order apply to the conduct of meetings only. They do not interpret laws or make up for deficiencies in bylaws or standing rules.

Minority Rights

While a democratic majority rule system may appear to be in conflict with minority rights, remember that there are higher laws that protect minority and individual rights. Nearly all nations have laws that protect the natural rights of all individuals, including the UN's Universal Declaration of Human Rights (UDHR). No group may make a decision that would violate universally recognized human rights and fundamental freedoms.

For Maximum Efficiency

Sharing the decision-making process in meetings is like driving a car. There are rules to be learned and skills to be attained. Once this has been done, group decision-making is second nature, like driving. If each member reads this book thoughtfully at least once, and if the chair does the same at least twice, and if members agree to follow these rules, your meetings should move as easily as the car of an experienced driver who can drive competently without wondering which pedal to press.

The Tenth Edition

The tenth edition, like each previous edition, has been revised to make the book clearer, more useful, and easier to work with. However, the rules of all editions are so similar that organizations can use earlier editions along with the latest edition without conflicts.

Virtual Meetings

These rules, modified if necessary, can be used for telephone or video conference meetings and for computer-connected meetings in which discussions and voting are done electronically.

To Adopt or Modify These Rules of Order

Add to the standing rules or bylaws a statement such as: "This organization's meetings shall be governed by Democratic Rules of Order." You could also add: "Members' general meetings shall be conducted by a formal chair, and the executive board's meetings shall be conducted by an informal chair" . Similarly, modifications can be made to these rules to make them conform to an organization's special needs.

An Impersonal Referee

These rules are complete. When adopted, they form the official rules of order for your organization's meetings. This book is your parliamentarian--or referee--when needed.

Governing Elements

Good governance has structure.

Government Control

The governments of some jurisdictions require that the constitution and bylaws of incorporated societies be approved by the members and that reports be submitted annually.

Constitution

A constitution is a short document stating the name and purpose of the organization. Changes to a constitution may require advance notice, a large majority of votes (e.g. two-thirds or three-quarters), a secret ballot, and/or government approval if the organization is incorporated. Indeed, some clauses may be unalterable, so an organization might have to be disbanded and reformed to change them. Many unincorporated organizations today are formed without constitutions and place all governing rules in their bylaws.

Bylaws

The governing rules of the organization, covering topics such as membership, officers, elections, duties, finances, meetings, quorum, discipline, amendments, and the seal. Changes to the bylaws may require advance notice,a large majority of votes (e.g. two-thirds or three-quarters), a secret ballot, and/or government approval.

Standing Rules

Standing rules are a record, usually in list form, of previously made decisions that provide future guidance. Standing rules can be changed by a majority of votes at any regular meeting, provided a quorum (the minimum number of members required to be present) is present.

Unless all members are present and none object, changes to an existing standing rule governing the conduct of members' meetings apply only to future meetings. Some organizations require advance notice before a decision listed in the standing rules can be changed.

Rules of Order

A set of rules, established by the standing rules or bylaws, by which the members agree to govern their meetings. This book supplies a complete set of rules that can be used by any organized group. Rules of order are subject always to the laws of the land, the constitution, the bylaws, and existing standing rules, any of which we call a *law* in this book.

Executive Board

A group of members elected for a limited time to conduct the organization's business in accordance with the members' wishes. Their responsibilities and limitations are specified in the bylaws. Their authority lies only with the whole board, and no single member should assume any special authority or responsibility unless such powers have been delegated to that individual by the board. When a person serves in a capacity such as "Director," "Strata Council Member," "Trustee," or "Governor," that person is still obligated to act in complete compliance with the will of the members.

Officers

President, vice president, secretary, treasurer, etc., elected by the members or appointed by the executive board for a limited time. Their responsibilities and limitations are specified in the bylaws. In some organizations, the officers form part or all of the executive board.

Election Procedures

Usually found in the bylaws and stating when elections are to be held, the requirements and terms of office, nominating and voting procedures, balloting, and the number and appointment of vote counters.

Members Making Decisions

It is easier to make good decisions when everyone knows the rules.

Final Authority

Given a quorum, the will of the majority of members present and voting at any meeting held in accordance with the bylaws is the final authority and cannot be thwarted by any individual or by any previous decision, except where a higher law provides an exception.

Equal Rights

Unless a law states differently, each member has one vote and an equal voice in all decisions.

The Chair

The president or someone elected by the members or appointed by the executive board to conduct the members' meetings.

Chair's Authority

The chair's duty is to preserve order and fairness in meetings by following the bylaws and rules of order. Members must abide by the rulings of the chair without debate except when a point of order is made.

Formal Chair

In large meetings, the chair must be--and must be seen to be--absolutely impartial. The chair must refrain from expressing personal opinions in words or gestures and should not participate in discussion except to guide it in an orderly fashion. If, on rare occasions, the chair has relevant, brief information, the chair may depart from this rule, but the chair must always avoid showing any bias. The chair cannot make a motion.

If the chair needs to participate actively in a discussion, arrangements should be made for another member to fill this position until the motion has been voted on. A member may call the chair to a point of order for wrongful participation, and the chair should comply with good spirit.

Informal Chair

In smaller or less formal meetings, members may have a bylaw, standing rule, or custom permitting the chair to participate in discussions with the same privileges as other members.

Addressing the Chair

Members must wait for permission (a verbal or nonverbal sign) from the chair before speaking. If several members stand at once, the chair selects one and notes who should be next. The others should sit until the speaker has finished; in large assemblies, the chair may require members wishing to speak to line up behind a microphone, or put their names on a list and wait their turn. A list of the order of speakers, preferably visible to all, is often useful, especially for virtual meetings.

Quorum

The minimum number of members required by a law to be present before decisions can be made at meetings. The chair must find out if a quorum is present before the meeting begins and be kept informed of any drop in numbers that might cause the loss of a quorum.The chair should warn the members if this is likely to occur. If a quorum is not present, the meeting may continue unofficially and should arrange, if possible, to get a quorum or to set the time of the next meeting.

Agenda

The items of business and the order in which they are to be discussed at meetings, generally prepared by the secretary with executive board approval, or, in smaller meetings, by the chair. The agenda should be made known to members beforehand. An agenda distributed in advance is particularly valuable for virtual meetings. The agenda can be changed by the members any time during the meeting except when another motion is on the floor (being considered by the members). The agenda change must be voted on if one or more members object. Agenda headings might include:

- Opening of the meeting and approval of the agenda
- Minutes of the previous meeting
- Correspondence and reports
- Business arising from minutes, correspondence, and reports
- Motions to be presented and new business
- Announcements
- Adjournment and closing

Motions and Decisions

Sometimes decisions are made by consensus in which the chair says "If there are no objections, then [the decision is described]," but otherwise all decisions are made with motions or resolutions in which a member says "I move [that some action be taken]." Before any motion can be considered, it must be seconded by another member; this prevents time being spent discussing an idea that has little chance of approval.

A new motion cannot be made until the motion on the floor has been withdrawn or voted on, except for those motions that directly affect the motion on the floor. Possible actions that would affect the motion on the floor would include:

- amendment to a motion
- postponement to a later date
- referral to another entity
- imposing a limit to speakers' time
- making changes to the voting procedure
- point of order

Unless a law specifically allows, a member must be present to make a motion, thus preserving the valuable mover's privilege. If the members have been notified already of a proposed motion, however, any member present can make the motion when it comes up on the agenda.

If the motion is clear, does not conflict with a law, and has been seconded, the chair or the secretary should read out the motion to make sure it is recorded correctly. Experienced movers sometimes have motions already written to give to the secretary. If possible, the motion should be worded affirmatively.

It is customary to allow the mover to speak to the motion first, and then again at the end of the discussion.

Notice of motion

A notice of motion can be made to members in writing or verbally during a meeting regarding a motion to be presented at a future meeting.

Special meeting

Unless a law states differently, those present at a special meeting can make decisions only on topics given in the notice calling that meeting.

Opinion poll (straw vote)

A nonbinding opinion poll (straw vote) can be held by the chair any time during a meeting if the members are willing. If a member objects, the chair should ask the members for a decision and conduct the opinion poll or not according to the members' vote.

Mover's Privilege

During discussion, ideas for improving the motion may occur. Provided that not more than one member objects, the mover may reword or withdraw the motion any time before it has been voted on. A seconder for new wording or withdrawal is required. Rewording can be continued until the motion is as perfect as the mover, assisted by the meeting, can make it.

Once the mover has decided on new wording--and it has been seconded--the chair or secretary should read out the reworded motion, which immediately becomes a new motion on the floor, replacing the previous one. If two members object prior to this reading out of the reworded motion, changes can be made only with motions to amend.

Amendments

If the mover does not--or cannot, because of objections--make a suggested change to the motion, any member may move an amendment to the original motion. An amendment may delete, substitute, or add words that will modify the original motion but must not negate it or change the intent.

The amendment, when accepted by the chair and seconded,

immediately becomes a new motion on the floor, temporarily replacing the original motion. The amendment grants mover's privilege to the mover of the amendment. Any rewording must be acceptable to the chair as not changing the topic. The details of the proposed amendment are discussed (not the original motion), and then the amendment is voted on. An amendment cannot be amended, but it can be defeated and replaced with another amendment.

If the amendment passes, the secretary should read the newly amended motion, which is now a new motion on the floor to be discussed (if desired) and voted on. It cannot be reworded or withdrawn by the mover's privilege now, since it has been partly established by the members, but this new motion can be passed, defeated, or amended again.

If the amendment fails, the previous motion again becomes the motion on the floor. If this previous motion was the original motion (having never been amended), then the original mover regains the mover's privilege. Further amendments are allowed, one at a time.

Postpone, Refer

A member may, any time before the motion has been voted on, move to **postpone** the motion on the floor (including any amendments passed) to an indefinite or a specific future occasion or to **refer** it to a standing committee, or an ad hoc committee specific for this purpose, for further study.

A member believing that consideration of a particular motion would be unwise could move "that we postpone the motion indefinitely." If the motion to **postpone indefinitely** is seconded and passed, then that particular motion cannot be discussed further at that meeting. It can be brought up at another meeting. A motion cannot be postponed permanently, because one meeting cannot bind a future meeting.

Voting

When all members who wish to speak have done so, the chair should call for a vote.Unless a larger majority is required , a decision is made (the motion is passed) when a quorum is present and more than half the votes are affirmative. Spoiled ballots and members not voting are not counted.

Calling for a vote

Members who believe discussion is complete sometimes call out "We are ready to vote," or the chair might ask "Are you ready to vote?" The response is a guide for the chair only and does not force a vote. A member who believes that the chair is calling for the vote too early or is delaying too long can rise on a point of order and move that "we delay the vote for more discussion" or that "we vote now." Such a motion needs seconding and should be voted on with little or no discussion.

Member's right to speak

Every member has a right to speak once to a motion, but in large meetings, a motion limiting speakers' times could be passed. The chair should not normally accept a motion to "vote now" if members who have not yet spoken are waiting to do so. However, if arguments on both sides of the question have been fairly presented and good order is being jeopardized by discussions becoming repetitive, the chair should accept such a motion.

After the members have decided to vote, either by general consensus or by passing a motion to vote, the chair or the secretary should read out the motion again, and the chair should make sure that all members understand it. Then the chair should call for the vote with "All in favor of the motion, please say 'yes' [or raise a hand]", "All opposed, say 'no' [or raise a hand]," or "Please mark your ballots now," etc. The chair must announce the result. If ballots need to be counted, the chair announces the results after the ballots are tallied.

How votes are taken

Custom or a standing rule usually determines how votes are taken. Some groups vote by voice, which makes it more difficult to tell which way others are voting; some groups vote by a show of hands, voting cards, standing, secret ballot, or roll call, all of which make it easier to count the votes. If the chair, assisted by the secretary, is uncertain which way the vote went, the chair can ask for a show of hands. If it is still unclear, the chair can ask for a standing vote, saying "Those in favor, please stand" (pause), "Please be seated. Those opposed, please stand" (pause), "Please be seated."

A member who believes that there has been a **miscount** can ask--or, if necessary, move--"that we repeat the count with a standing [or ballot] vote." If this motion is seconded and passed, then the vote must be taken again. Motions can be made requiring that a vote be by ballot, that the counted ballots be destroyed, that the number of votes for and against be announced, or that some other action be taken regarding the vote.

Absentee voting

Unless a law specifically allows proxy or absentee voting, a member must be present to vote, either in person or virtually.

Ethics

A member who would benefit personally from a decision may participate in the discussion but should voluntarily refrain from voting.

Tie Vote

A tie vote means the motion has not passed. Members might wish to reconsider it immediately, or at a future time. In some organizations, an already existing law gives the chair an extra vote to break a tie.

Larger Majority Vote

A mover who believes that the action being proposed needs strong support from many members may finish the motion with wording such as: "… and that this motion require a three-quarters [or some other ratio] affirmative vote to pass." A simple majority of members could easily remove this special requirement with an amendment; therefore, if this restriction is not removed through an amendment, the larger majority vote requirement has been accepted by the meeting and is now needed for the motion to pass. Sometimes a law will already exist requiring a larger majority vote on certain financial matters, bylaw changes, or other matters of import.

Informal Discussion

Occasionally, there is merit in discussing an idea informally before a motion has been formulated. To allow for this, a member may move "that we discuss [some topic] informally for a few minutes." This motion needs seconding and should be voted on almost immediately. After discussing the topic, if no motion is forthcoming, the meeting should proceed with the next item on the agenda.

Rescind

Unless a law makes an exception, and providing it would not create a breach of contract, a motion to rescind (repeal) a previous decision requires only a majority to pass and can be made at a time when the agenda allows (normally under new business or resulting from a point of order changing the agenda).

Reconsider

A motion to reconsider a previous decision can be made immediately after the decision has been made or at any meeting during new business or when it has been put on the agenda (perhaps by a point of order). It should be voted on immediately with little or no discussion. If the motion to reconsider is passed, then a member moves the previous motion or a replacement motion on the same topic, and it is again discussed and voted on. The mover's privilege applies. The new decision replaces the previous one. A motion can be reconsidered as often as the members are willing . Once the decision to reconsider has been made, no new business can be done until the reconsideration has been dealt with.

Minutes

Minutes are records of meetings, kept by the secretary. They should include at least all major events and motions. The secretary should maintain a filing system for minutes, reports, correspondence, etc.

After the minutes of the previous meeting have been circulated or read to all members, the chair should ask if there are any corrections. After any corrections have been made, the chair should ask "All in favor of adopting the minutes as circulated [or read, or corrected], please say 'yes' [or raise a hand]" (pause), "All opposed, please say 'no' [or raise a hand]" and then announce the decision. Once adopted, and signed by the chair and secretary, the minutes are an official record generally acceptable in a court of law.

Reports

Executive boards, committees, and individuals often report recommendations or give other information to the members at meetings.

After a report containing information has been read to the meeting, no motion is necessary. However, in some groups it is customary to finish with "I move that this report be **received** as read," which means that the members have heard and understood the report.

If the report contains a recommendation, the person presenting the report might move that "this report be adopted as read." This motion means that the members have agreed with and **adopted** the report and its recommendations. Of course, a member could propose an amendment changing "adopted" to "received," so that the members would not be bound by the report's recommendations. Treasurers' reports are usually received, rather than adopted, as the members are not in a position to guarantee the report's accuracy.

Ratifying a Previous Decision

If a decision was made, perhaps due to an emergency, that exceeded the authority of the member, committee, or meeting at the time it was made, this decision can be either ratified or not by the members who do have the authority at a later meeting. This is done by a member making a motion to ratify the decision. Normally, the motion to ratify is quickly passed. However, if the motion to ratify is not passed, this is a **non-confidence** vote. Unless a higher law (e.g. a bylaw) has provided for this in a different way, the member or group that made the decision in question must resign and an election be called to have them replaced.

Adjournment

If a bylaw or standing rule requires adjournment by a specified time, the chair should warn the members as that time draws near, so that they can either finish quickly or extend the meeting with a motion, if it is allowed. If the meeting has not been extended, the chair should declare the meeting adjourned at the specified time. Otherwise, the chair could say, "Since the business is finished, if there are no objections" (pause), "the meeting is adjourned." Or the chair could say, "Since the business is finished, let's adjourn; all in favor, please say 'yes' " (pause), "All opposed, please say 'no.' " If the motion passes, the chair then says "The meeting is adjourned."

Keeping Meetings Flowing

A productive meeting needs good order.

Staying on the Subject

Members must discuss only one topic or motion at a time. If necessary, the chair should interrupt a speaker to insist that this rule be obeyed. If ideas are brought up that may be valuable but are off topic, a "Parking Lot" concept can be used. The chair or secretary records the ideas to be brought up later for discussion at an appropriate time, perhaps as a new business agenda item for a future meeting.

More Thought, Less Talk

A member must not take more than a fair share of floor time nor speak more than once on a motion until all others who wish to do so have had a turn. Exceptions may occur, however, with new information or a series of questions and answers involving useful facts. If necessary, members could pass a motion or have a standing rule, starting next meeting, limiting each speaker's time and appointing a timekeeper to enforce it.

Mutual Respect

Members must respect the rights of other members to have their own quiet judgment on issues. Decisions should be based on consideration of facts rather than on the skill of the speakers or one person's opinion of how others should vote. Members should speak to contribute light only, not heat!

Members must not use any form of personal criticism or ridicule to sway opinions. A member may criticize an idea, but never a fellow member. A member must never interject or interfere with another member's right to an uninterrupted floor when speaking, except as allowed under a point of order. The chair should insist that this rule be followed.

Point of Order

A member who believes that a law or the meeting's good order is being breached may rise at any time and say, "Mister/Madam Chair, point of order." The chair should immediately acknowledge this member, who should then briefly explain why he or she believes a law or good order is being breached. The chair then rules on the point, either correcting the situation or explaining why it is in order.

If the chair declares that the situation is in order, the member may exercise **one last option** by rising and saying "Mister/Madam Chair, I request a vote on this point of order." First the member, and then the chair, briefly explain their reasons. Then with little or no further discussion, the chair calls for a vote, saying "All who believe that [this action] conforms to our rules [or good order], please say 'yes' [or raise a hand]" (pause), "Those who disagree, please say 'no' [or raise a hand]." The chair and the member raising the point of order must abide by this vote.

Disturbances

Filibustering (intentionally delaying progress by prolonged speaking) or any other action that interferes with good order is not allowed. If a member is speaking too long, the chair should give a polite reminder. If the member continues, the chair can interrupt and request a decision from the meeting with "I request a decision from the meeting. All wishing this member to stop speaking now, please say 'yes' [or raise a hand]" (pause), "All opposed, please say 'no' [or raise a hand]." If the decision was for the member to stop speaking, the chair says, "Sir/Madam, the members wish you to stop speaking now. Please do so." Or if the decision was opposed, "Sir/Madam, the members are willing for you to continue. Please do so."

If a member or group of members does not stop speaking. when asked by the chair or a motion has been passed by the members, then the chair can interrupt the speaker and ask for a motion requiring the speaker(s) to leave the meeting or, if necessary, for a motion to adjourn the meeting to reconvene at a later time. Only the members can make such a decision. Physical force should not be used against a member, although the speaker's microphone could be turned off on request of the chair.

Differing Opinions

If there is a difference over the meaning of a bylaw or a procedure, etc., the chair may assist in solving the dispute. For example, the chair could pose a question designed to resolve the dispute and ask for a show of hands on it. The final decision rests with the members.

A New Chair

Serving as chair need not be a dreaded job; the rules in this book are straightforward, and your fellow members can assist you, if needed. You can let it be known that you appreciate help. Ask members to call out if they can't hear you and to remind you if you forget something. You could suggest "If you see ways I can chair the meetings more efficiently, please ask the secretary to give me a copy of the rules of order in which you have highlighted the points I most need to review."

As well as studying the bylaws, standing rules, and rules of order beforehand, it is helpful to study the agenda and perhaps to annotate it with reminders and notes so you won't forget them during the meeting. By the way, starting meetings on time is a valuable habit.

Committees and Small Meetings

Meetings can be both informal and orderly.

Committees

A committee is a group of one or more persons appointed by the executive board or the members to perform a continuing or short-term function. A **standing committee** is permanent until disbanded, although its membership may be changed periodically.An **ad hoc committee** is appointed to do a specific task and is temporary. The chair of a committee is appointed by the members or the executive board, or is elected from within the committee. Unless otherwise stated, the quorum of a committee or meeting is a majority of its members. Written guidelines are often used to provide order and continuity.

Less Formality

In committees and small meetings, the chair participates informally as a leader--subject always to the law and the will of the meeting, which in turn is responsible to the appointing body. The following is a list of examples of meeting types, in order of increasing degrees of formality:

- work parties making decisions by consensus led by the chair
- small meetings making minor decisions by consensus that are announced by the chair and recorded in minutes
- meetings of executive boards with an agenda and motions that are seconded, voted on, announced by the chair, and recorded in minutes by a secretary

Special Committees

Most committees are democratic, but sometimes a nondemocratic committee is formed in which one person has full responsibility, although others may help.

Chairing a Committee Meeting

Ideally, a committee brings to bear upon a subject the combined experience and wisdom of several people. But sometimes well-meaning people talk too much or too forcefully, quite unaware of how much time this wastes and how unfair it is to others. Meetings must be protected from such imbalance. The chair should not allow any member to be overly dominant.

The chair should assist members in sticking to the business at hand. (Socializing can be done before or after the meeting.) Light good humor is great, but should be brief. Replies to divergent opinions should be controlled and not allowed to degenerate into arguments.Facts should be allowed to speak for themselves. A little silence during a meeting--as members ponder a situation--is often the sign of an effective group.

When an idea needs to be written down or a letter produced, most committees find that these are better written and corrected by one or two people and then presented to the whole committee for final review.

In all meetings--of any size--the ideal is for members to seek the best solutions *together, as a unit,* rather than having sides debate to have their own viewpoints adopted. (True for legislative assemblies too, if only they applied it!)

Nondemocratic Meetings

Some meetings (such as a sales meeting in which a manager is instructing personnel) are not intended to be democratic, yet orderliness and respect for every individual and the employment of the basic principles of democratic rules will improve the efficiency of any meeting. Including a little democratic decision-making, when possible, usually brightens a meeting, making it more interesting for all participants.

PART 2 Further Help

Frequently Asked Questions

Involving the Chair

Q1.What qualities does the chair most need?

A1.Self-control, good humor, and a thorough knowledge of the constitution, the bylaws, the standing rules, and the rules of order of the organization.

Q2.What can a chair do to ensure a fair and harmonious discussion of a contentious item?

A2.If necessary, the chair can remind members:

• that the rules by which they have agreed to be governed allow them to discuss and make joint decisions in an orderly fashion, even when opinions are strongly divided

• that a member's right to an uninterrupted floor includes freedom from any kind of audience response while that member is speaking

• that a member who has spoken once may not reply to other speakers' statements--no matter how outrageous--until all others who wish to speak have done so

• that a member must be acknowledged by the chair before speaking

• that we need not change our opinions, but we must accept the voting majority as the authorized decision-maker

It may be helpful to have copies of this book on hand; members could be allowed to borrow one, and return it at the end of the meeting, so that appropriate sections can be referred to. If necessary, the chair should respectfully insist that these rules, especially those on pages 29 to 30 (Keeping Meetings Flowing), be followed.

Q3. How should the chair deal with confrontational, angry members?

A3. The most effective way is to not react even a little, to be calm, objective, proactive, and aware that remaining polite and dispassionate will help keep the situation controlled. Compassion for people less able to control their emotions sometimes helps a chair from dropping to the same level. It gets easier with experience.

Q4. Can the chair vote?

A4. Yes, unless a law states differently.

However, a formal chair should do so as inconspicuously as possible to avoid showing bias.

Q5. If both the chair and the vice-chair are absent, what happens?

A5. Any member, perhaps the secretary, can call the meeting to order, call for nominations, and conduct an election of a temporary chair for that meeting.

Q6. Should the chair guide the discussion?

A6. An occasional verbal summary can be helpful, but a formal chair must be careful to maintain impartiality.

A chair who keeps the discussion on track, prevents overzealous members from dominating, helps members speak clearly one at a time, and keeps the meeting from dragging on with repetitions, is doing much to make the meeting worthwhile. With direction from the chair, minor decisions can be made by consensus. For example, the chair might say, “Unless there is an objection, we will continue this meeting without the noisy microphone.”

Involving the Secretary

Q7.How detailed should minutes be?

A7.As detailed as the secretary and/or the members wish. Minutes should contain all motions exactly as passed and a very brief description of all major actions.Minutes often look like expanded agendas. Minutes of formal meetings will generally be fuller than those of informal meetings. Minutes of informal meetings might be simply a dated list of events and decisions.

Q8.Must the minutes include the names of the mover and seconder?

A8.No, but in more formal meetings, the secretary may wish to include them, or the members could pass a motion requiring that this be done.

Q9. Must the minutes of the previous meeting be read at the beginning of the meeting?

A9.Not necessarily;if the minutes have already been circulated (either before the meeting or at the beginning of the meeting), members may not wish to have them read aloud. The members determine the agenda .

Q10. When minutes of the previous meeting have been corrected, must the secretary rewrite them?

A10. Normally, corrections are made in the text or margin of the secretary's copy of the minutes and initialed by the chair and the secretary. However, if the secretary wishes, or if the members pass such a motion, then the minutes should be rewritten and the new copy be signed by the chair and the secretary. For virtual meetings, the minutes may be signed and transmitted electronically with the date of changes noted.

Q11. If the minutes of a previous meeting have been adopted and are later found to contain an error, what should be done?

A11. Once a meeting's minutes have been adopted and signed, that signed copy cannot be changed. Corrections should be noted and approved by the members in the later meeting and included in that meeting's minutes. Then a note of the later correction should be made on, or attached to, the original minutes, dated, and signed by the chair and secretary. For virtual meetings, any corrections to minutes can be made electronically with the changes dated.

Q12. Can a secretary make a motion?

A12. Any member except a formal chair can make a motion. However, in large meetings, it is usual for motions to be made from the floor.

Motions and Other Topics

Q13. Can a motion be put on the agenda without naming a mover?

A13. Yes. When its turn comes on the agenda, any member can move it. If the motion is not moved, the meeting proceeds on to the next item on the agenda.

Q14. What are the advantages of the mover's privilege?

A14. When members are cooperative, the mover's privilege enables them to improve a motion in an easy, natural way. Efficiency increases with experience. Since objection from any two members requires a more formal amending process, this privilege cannot be abused.

Q15. Can a member speak and vote against his or her own motion?

A15. Yes. The only restrictions on members' participation are those on pages 29 to 30 (Keeping Meetings Flowing). However, it may be wiser to modify the motion with the mover's privilege or an amendment.

Q16. Can a member who will be absent submit a written amendment to a motion that is on the agenda?

A16. No, unless a higher law allows. However, the member could submit a motion for the agenda that addresses the issue. It would need to be moved and seconded at the meeting to proceed. In a virtual meeting, the moving and seconding could be done electronically. The absent member would be made aware of the decision through the minutes.

Q17. Can the members add or change a standing rule during the meeting to give the chair a tie-breaking vote?

A17. No. They can change the standing rule, but it will not take effect until the next meeting because the meeting is governed by the existing standing rules. This rule protects the right of members not present at a particular meeting from having a major rule changed during that meeting--when they are not there to participate in the decision. However, if all members are present and none object, a standing rule could be changed immediately.

Q18. Our quorum is 40. Forty members were present. On a vote, there were eight affirmative votes, seven negative votes, and one spoiled ballot that did not contain a "yes" or a "no."

Twenty-four members did not vote. Did the motion pass?

A18. Yes. Two conditions are necessary for a motion to pass:

(1) The total number of members present must be at least a quorum.

(2) A majority of the legitimate votes cast must be affirmative.

In this case, both conditions were met. A quorum of members was present. The spoiled ballot did not count. Eight votes were a majority of the 15 legitimate votes cast.

Q19. What if a member feels an intermission would be helpful?

A19. The member can raise a point of order and move that members take a break and reassemble at a stated time.

Q20. Can an agenda be changed during a meeting to include a particular topic considered earlier?

A20. Yes. At a convenient time, a member can raise a point of order (assuming the proposed change will improve the good order of the meeting) and move the change in the agenda.

Q21. When can a motion that has been postponed indefinitely be brought up again?

A21. At a future meeting, at a time when the agenda allows (normally under new business or resulting from a point of order changing the agenda).

Q22. Our bylaws require a notice of motion in order to spend over $1,000 at any meeting. A notice of motion to install an electronic security system for $5,000 was properly sent to

each member. During the meeting this motion was changed; the decision was made to purchase better locks instead, for $4,000. Is this acceptable?

A22. Yes. The amount is within the financial limit established by the notice of motion, and the motion is on the same topic of security. If there were a difference of opinion on this, the chair could ask "If you agree with my decision to accept this motion as being in accord with the notice of motion, please raise your hand" (pause), "If opposed, please raise your hand," thereby emphasizing that the members are the final authority.

However, changing the motion (by means of the mover's privilege or an amendment) to purchasing a system for $5,200 would not be acceptable, as the amount is over the limit established by the notice of motion. Similarly, changing the motion to purchasing a sound system for $5,000 would not be acceptable, as the topic is different.

Q23. How can we have a relaxed, interactive "think tank" session, with maximum freedom to explore new, problem-solving ideas in an orderly way?

A23. Use the informal discussion rule to free the meeting from formality. Then appoint the chair or a member to act as a neutral facilitator to be sure that every idea presented is received with complete absence of pre-judgment on its merit so that no one is reluctant to mention a "far-out" idea. You could also appoint the secretary or a member as a recorder to list the ideas on a board or chart so that none are lost.

Large meetings sometimes break into smaller groups, each with its own facilitator and recorder. When the session is finished, the groups come together and hear reports from the facilitators. Ideas originating from these sessions may lead to motions.

Q24. Can you give an example of an acceptable and an unacceptable amendment?

A24. Consider this motion: "I move that wego to Sam's restaurant next time."

Amendment #1: "I move that we amend this motion by replacing the word 'Sam's' with 'The Golden Pagoda.'" This is acceptable, because it does not negate the motion or change the topic.

Amendment #2: "I move that we amend this motion by adding the word 'not' in front of the word 'go.'" This is not acceptable, because it negates the original motion.

The same result could be achieved more simply by defeating the original motion.

Q25. What is a vote by roll call?

A25. The secretary calls the name of each member, who then votes audibly. Each member's vote is recorded on a list.

Q26. What is a resolution?

A26. A resolution is a formal expression of the meeting's opinion on some topic, or a resolve to take some action worded in a special way. It usually consists of a preamble containing one or more premises followed by a conclusion. For example: "I move that we adopt the following resolution: **Whereas**(followed by one or more premises), **therefore, be it resolved that** (followed by a resolve)." Of course, the members can change any part with the mover's privilege or amendments before voting on the whole motion.

Q27. What is an example of an opinion poll (straw vote)?

A27. While considering the purchase of a new computer, a member wanted to know how many members would make use of it and asked the chair to find out. The chair said "If there are no objections, we will have a show of hands on this question (pause). How many would use this computer if we buy it?" Then the chair announced the result. If a member had objected to this poll, the chair would have asked "All willing for this meeting to conduct this poll, please say 'yes'"(pause); "All opposed, please say 'no.'" The chair would then have conducted the poll or not as the meeting decided.

Q28. Can you give an example of how a higher law would modify a rule of order?

A28. The rule on equal rights gives each member one vote. However, in some jurisdictions, laws governing meetings of condominium owners give each member one vote for each condominium unit owned by that member. A member owning five units in the condominium complex has five votes. Similarly in a corporation's shareholders' meeting, votes are usually proportional to the number of voting shares owned.

Another example would be the rule on a tie vote. In some jurisdictions, for example in some condominium owners' bylaws,

laws governing meetings give the chair of the meeting a tie-breaking vote in addition to the chair's original vote.

Q29. Our board spent $7,000 on repairs to an elevator, claiming it was an emergency; but their spending limit was $2,000. Were they in order?

A29. Yes. However, at the next regular or special meeting, the members must ratify this expenditure. Usually this motion is passed. If the motion to ratify the expenditure is not passed, then the members have lost confidence in that board, and an election must be called to have them replaced.

Q30. Will these rules work in conventions, conferences, and legislative assemblies?

A30. Yes, they will work well in conjunction with the specific procedures and rules dealing with agendas, delegates, speaking orders and limits, voting methods,and the many details involved in the smooth operation of such events.

It is easy to modify these rules of order with a standing rule or bylaw to make them conform to special needs.

Q31. Can a formal president present a motion to the meeting?

A31. A chair can arrange for another member to present the motion if he or she is willing to stay uninvolved. Otherwise, the chair can ask the vice president, secretary, or another member to chair the meeting throughout this discussion and voting while she participates from the floor as a regular member.

Q32. What can members do if they notice a bias in a

chair or committee?

A32. A member can raise a point of order and insist that the chair (or committee) allow fair discussion of both sides of an issue. If there is formal chair, members must insist that the chair be impartial.

Sample Meeting

The following is an example of a meeting governed by the rules laid out in this book. This script of an imaginary meeting contains examples of how the rules work in awkward situations. Before reading it, we suggest you first read the Rules in Part 1 and the Frequently Asked Questions thoroughly to see that the rules are mostly common sense. Then this sample meeting will be more useful.

C = Chair

M = Member

C: Welcome! Let's open our meeting.

Are there any changes to the agenda? M1?

M1: I move that consideration of a fish pond be deleted from the agenda.

M2: I second the motion.

C: It has been moved and seconded that consideration of a

fish pond be deleted from the agenda.

[Discussion]

C: Are you ready to vote now?

[Members call out "Let's vote now"]

C: Since we are ready to vote, will the secretary please read the motion.

[Secretary reads the motion]

C: All in favor of deleting the fish pond from the agenda, please raise a hand. ... All opposed, please raise a hand. ... Thank you. The vote is tied.

There are 40 affirmative votes and 40 negative votes, so the motion did not pass, and the agenda remains unchanged. The minutes of our last meeting have been circulated. Are there any changes or omissions? Yes, M3?

M3: The meeting started at 7:30, not 8:00 p.m.

C: Thank you M3. If there are no objections (pause), will the secretary please make that correction now. Are there further corrections? ... All in favor of adopting the minutes as corrected, please raise a hand. ... All opposed, please raise a hand. ... Thank you. The minutes have been adopted as corrected, and the secretary and I will sign them now.

C: The next item on the agenda is a report from the executive board, to be read by M4.

[M4 reads the report]

M4: I move that this report be adoptedas read.

M5: I second the motion.

C: It has been moved and seconded that the report be adopted as read. M6?

M6: I don't think we should be bound by this report's recommendation that we change our management company.

I suggest that M4 replace the word "adopted" with the word "received."

C: M4, are you willing to make that change?

M4: No. I do not wish to make that change.

C: Yes, M6?

M6: I move that we amend this motion by replacing the word "adopted" with the word "received."

M7: I second the motion.

C: It has been moved and seconded that we amend this motion by replacing the word "adopted" with the word "received" to prevent the members from being bound by the report's recommendations.

[Discussion]

[Members call out "Let's vote now"]

C: If there are no objections, we will vote now. All in favor of the amendment changing the word "adopted" to the word "received," please raise a hand. … All opposed, please raise a hand. … Thank you. The amendment did not pass, and now we must consider the original, unchanged, motion. Is there any further discussion? Since there is none, let's vote. All in favor of adopting the report as read, please raise a hand. … All opposed, please raise a hand. …

Thank you. The motion to adopt has been passed.

M8: Ms. Chair. Point of order.

C: Yes, M8?

M8: That vote was so close. I request we vote again by ballot.

C: I am satisfied the vote was correct. M8?

M8: Well, I am not satisfied, and I move that we vote again by ballot!

M9: I second the motion.

C: All in favor of voting again by ballot, please stand and remain standing until I say "thank you." Will the secretary please help me count? … Thank you. All opposed, please stand. Secretary, please help count again. … Thank you. The motion to vote again by ballot has been lost, 37 affirmative and 43 negative. So the original motion to adopt M4's report with its recommendations remains passed. The next item on the agenda is the fish pond. M10?

M10: I move that we informally discuss the idea of a new fish pond for a few minutes now.

M11: I second the motion.

C: All in favor of informally discussing the fish pond now please raise a hand. … All opposed please raise a hand.… Thank you. The motion has been passed, so we will now discuss this topic together informally.

[Informal discussion]

M12: Since we are not ready to make a motion on this

topic yet, I move that we continue with the agenda now.

M13: I second the motion.

C: All in favor of continuing with the agenda now, please raise a hand. … All opposed, please raise a hand. … Thank you. The motion has been passed. The next item arising from the minutes is the notice of motion made at our last meeting about painting our building. M14?

M14: Because I believe this motion should have strong support from a large majority of members, it contains a special requirement. I move that we have all the exterior wood of our building painted at a cost not to exceed $20,000 and that this motion require a 75 percent affirmative vote to pass.

M15: I second the motion.

C: Since members have been notified, this motion complies with our bylaws and is in order. Would the secretary please read it.

[Secretary reads the motion]

C: M14, do you wish to speak to your motion?

[M14 speaks to the motion]

[Discussion]

M14: After hearing the discussion, I wish to reword my motion to read: that we have the exterior window frames of our building painted at a cost not to exceed $10,000, and that this motion require a 75% affirmative vote to pass.

M16: I second the motion.

M17: I object to this change in the motion.

M18: I also object to this change in the motion.

C: Since there have been two objections, this motion cannot be changed with the mover's privilege, and the original motion is still the motion on the floor. M14?

M14: I move that we amend the motion by replacing the words "all the wood on the exterior of our building" with "the exterior window frames" and the price of "$20,000" with "$10,000."

M19: I second the amendment.

C: The amendment is in order. Would the secretary please read the amendment to be sure we have it written correctly?

[Secretary reads the amendment]

C: The mover of the amendment may speak first.

[Discussion]

[Members call out "Let's vote now"]

C: Hearing no objection, let's vote now. Will the secretary please read the amendment?

[Secretary reads the amendment]

C: All in favor of the amendment, please raise a hand. … All opposed, please raise a hand. … Thank you. A majority are in favor, and the amendment has been passed. The newly amended motion is now the motion on the floor. Would the secretary please read this new motion?

[Secretary reads the motion]

[Discussion]

C: Is there any further discussion? Will the secretary please read the new motion again before we vote on it?

[Secretary reads the motion]

C: Does everyone understand what we are voting on? ... To make counting easy, we will have a standing vote. All in favor of the motion, please stand. ... All opposed, please stand. ...Thank you.

There were 48 affirmative votes and 32 negative votes, which means 60 percent are affirmative. The motion required 75% to pass. It has been lost. M20?

M20: I move that we reconsider this motion.

M21: I second the motion.

C: All in favor of reconsidering the motion, please raise a hand. ... All opposed, please raise a hand. ... A majority is in favor, and the motion to reconsider has been passed. M22?

M22: With a slight modification, I think this idea might gain approval. I move that we have the exterior window frames and doors of the building painted at a cost not to exceed $15,000 and that this motion require a 75% affirmative vote to pass.

M23: I second the motion.

C: Would the secretary please read the motion.

[Secretary reads the motion]

[Discussion]

C: M24?

M24: Ms. Chair, I move we vote now.

M25: I second the motion.

C: As soon as M26, who was waiting to speak, has had his turn, I will accept your motion.

M26: Thank you.

[M26 speaks.]

C: It has been moved and seconded that we vote now.

M28: Ms. Chair, point of order. Several more of us would like to speak to this motion.

C: Both sides of the question have been fairly presented during the past 20 minutes. Over 80 members are present.We will let the members decide.All in favor of voting now, please raise a hand. … All opposed, please raise a hand. … Thank you. The motion is carried and we will vote now. Secretary, please read the motion once again.

[Secretary reads the motion]

C: Thank you. We will have a standing vote. All in favor, please stand. … Thank you. All opposed, please stand.… Thank you. There were 60 affirmative votes and 20 negative votes. The number of affirmative votes was 75% of the total votes, so the motion has been passed. The executive board can now have this work done. Next on our agenda is new business. M29?

M29: I move that we reconsider this last motion.

M30: I second the motion.

C: All in favor of reconsidering this last motion, please raise a hand. … All opposed, please raise a hand. … The motion to reconsider has been lost.

M30: I move that we reconsider this last motion.

M29: I second the motion.

C: This motion is out of order as we have already made a decision on it. M30?

M30: Ms. Chair. It is not out of order, as our rules of order state on page 27 that "A motion can be reconsidered as often as the members are willing."

C: The members have just decided that they are not willing to reconsider this motion, so we will now proceed with new business. M31?

M31: My condominium is next to the games room, and players are frequently noisy. I move that this room be closed daily at 9:00 p.m.

C: Is there a seconder for the motion?The motion fails for lack of a seconder. M32?

M32: I move that we post a sign in the games room asking players to be quiet after 9:00 p.m.

M33: I second the motion.

C: It has been moved and seconded that we post a sign in the games room requesting players to be quiet after 9:00 p.m. Is there any discussion?

M34: The motion should put a limit on the cost of this sign.

C: M32?

M32: Good idea. I would like to change my motion to read that the maintenance committee be asked to spend up to $45 for a sign in the games room requesting players to be

quiet after 9:00 p.m.

M33: I second the new motion.

M35: I object to this change in M32's original motion.

C: Since there is only one objection, this change is acceptable. Will the secretary please read the new motion.

[Secretary reads the motion]

C: M36?

M36: Because there are other factors to be considered, I move that we refer this motion to the executive board for their consideration and ask them to report back to us at our next meeting.

M37: I second the motion.

[Discussion]

C: Anyone else? … It has been moved and seconded that we refer this motion to the executive board and ask them to report back to us at our next meeting. All in favor, please raise a hand. … All opposed, please raise a hand. … The motion is carried. Is there any further new business? M38?

M38: Three meetings ago we decided to carpet the foyer. Nothing has been done. I move that we rescind the motion to carpet the foyer!

M34: I second the motion.

M39: Ms. Chair. Point of order.

C: Go ahead, M39.

M39: The contract has been given to a firm. By our rules of order we cannot rescind that motion.

C: I believe you are right, M39. We cannot rescind a motion if doing so would create a breach of contract. M38?

M38: The color is wrong! The price is too high! We are not breaking a contract! It hasn't been signed yet! I insist that we--

M39: I agree with--

C: Hold on a minute, M39! Please wait until you have been acknowledged before speaking.

M38: Ms. Chair. Point of order.

C: Yes, M38.

M38: I believe this motion is in order and request a vote on this point of order.

C: Thank you, M38. Please explain your reasoning. Then I will explain my reasoning, and then we will vote.

[M38 explains]

[C responds]

C: Now the members will decide. All who believe that this motion to rescind is out of order, please raise a hand. … All opposed, please raise a hand. … Thank you. The motion has been carried.The motion to rescind has been considered out of order, and we will now proceed to the next item of business.

[More business is discussed]

C: Our standing rules require us to adjourn by 10:00 p.m. We have only ten minutes left. M40?

M40: I move that we change that standing rule to read: "that we adjourn at 10:00 p.m. or at a later time if the

members attending so wish."

M41: I second the motion.

C: This motion, if passed, will not affect tonight's closing time as we are governed by our existing standing rule. The motion before us is that we change our standing rule to read that "we adjourn at 10:00 p.m. or at a later time if the members attending so wish."

[Short discussion]

[Members call out "Let's vote now"]

C: Secretary, please read the motion.

[Secretary reads the motion]

C: If there is no objection, we will vote now. All in favor, please raise a hand. … All opposed, please raise a hand. … The motion has been carried and will allow members to extend the time of adjournment at future meetings. It is now 10:00 p.m., and I declare this meeting adjourned!

Flowchart

Using *Democratic Rules of Order*

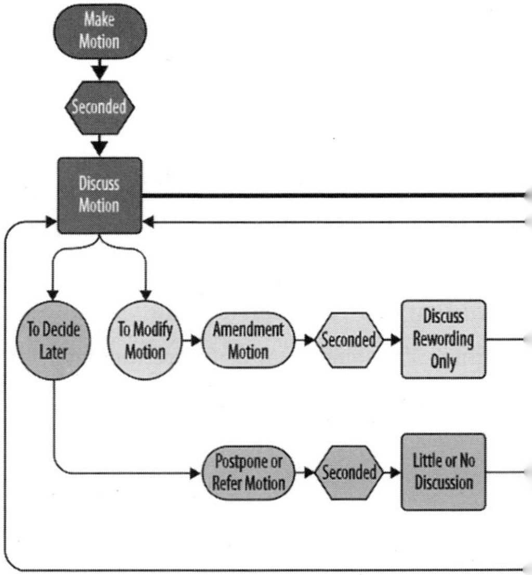

Good Order

·stay on topic

·One speaker at a time, acknowledged by chair

·No interrupting

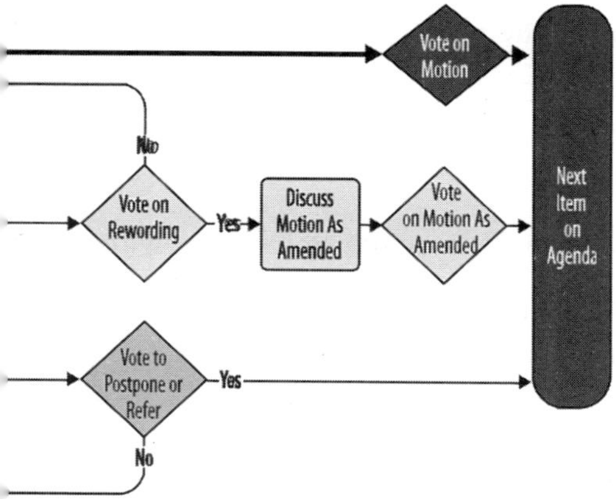

Point of Order

·Member explains how a law or good order is being breached

·Chair rules on point of order

·Vote if necessary

Summary of the Rules

Fairness (equal rights of members) and good order are the underlying principles .

The **final authority is the majority of voting members**, provided a quorum is present, subject always to any applicable higher law (a law of the land, a constitution, a bylaw, or an existing standing rule) .

In **formal meetings**, the chair guides impartially without taking part in discussion. In informal meetings, the chair participates as an equal member.

A **motion** should be worded affirmatively and must not conflict with any higher law.Each motion requires a seconder.

The **mover's privilege** allows the mover to reword or withdraw the motion provided there is a seconder and not more than one member objects .

Amendments can delete, substitute, or add words to a motion on the floor but must not negate it or change its topic. An amendment cannot be amended.

Postpone, refer: A motion can be postponed to an indefinite or a specific future occasion or referred to a committee for further study.

Voting: Common voting methods include voting by ballot, standing, show of hands, show of voting cards, and voice. For a motion to pass, a quorum must be present, and more than half the votes cast must be affirmative .

Informal discussion: A motion to informally discuss some topic, if passed, allows members to consider an idea without the formality of a motion .

Rescind, reconsider: A previous decision can be rescinded or reconsidered by the members at any appropriate time.

Ratify a previous decision: A decision exceeding the authority of a member, committee or meeting can be ratified at a later meeting.

Good order: Members should discuss only one motion at a time. A member must not take more than a fair share of floor time nor interrupt another member except as allowed with a point of order.

Point of order: A member who believes that a law or the meeting's good order is being breached may rise immediately and say "point of order." The chair should allow the member to explain and, if necessary, should call for a vote for a decision .